THE TROLL HOLE MUSEUM
Coloring Book for Adults

Sherry Groom

BALBOA.
PRESS

A DIVISION OF HAY HOUSE

Balboa Press books may be ordered through booksellers or by contacting:

Balboa Press
A Division of Hay House
1663 Liberty Drive
Bloomington, IN 47403
www.balboapress.com
1 (877) 407-4847

ISBN: 978-1-9822-0627-7 (sc)
ISBN: 978-1-9822-0626-0 (e)

Library of Congress Control Number: 2018901408

Print information available on the last page.

Balboa Press rev. date: 06/20/2018

THE TROLL HOLE

MUSEUM

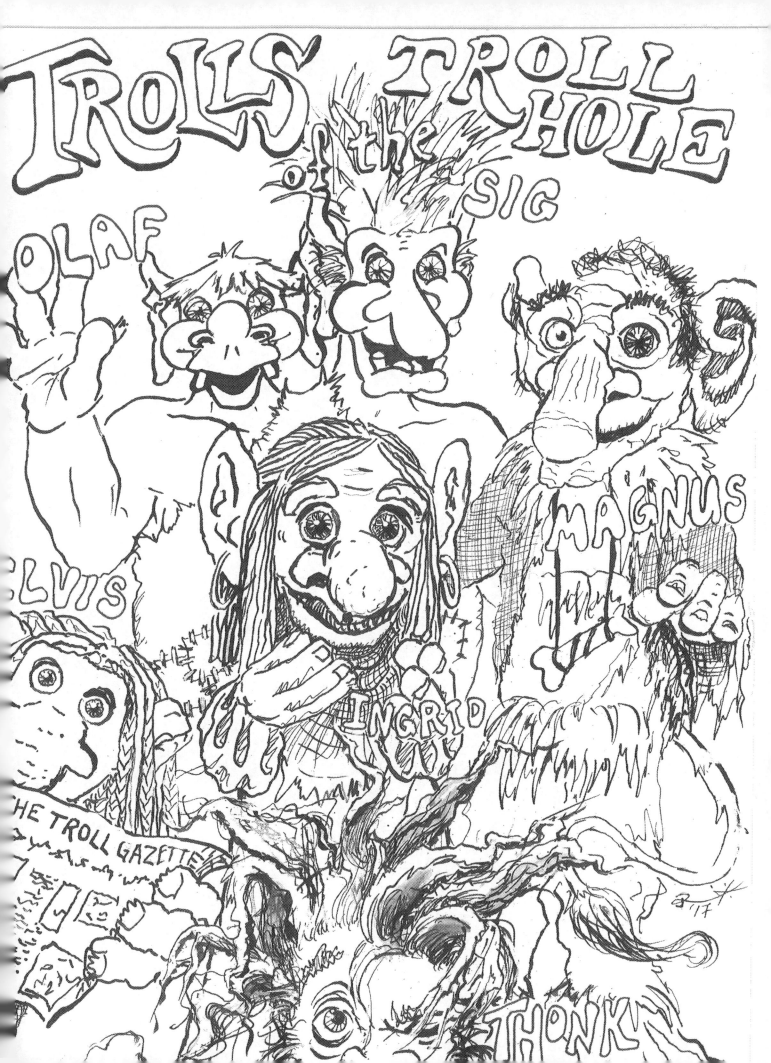

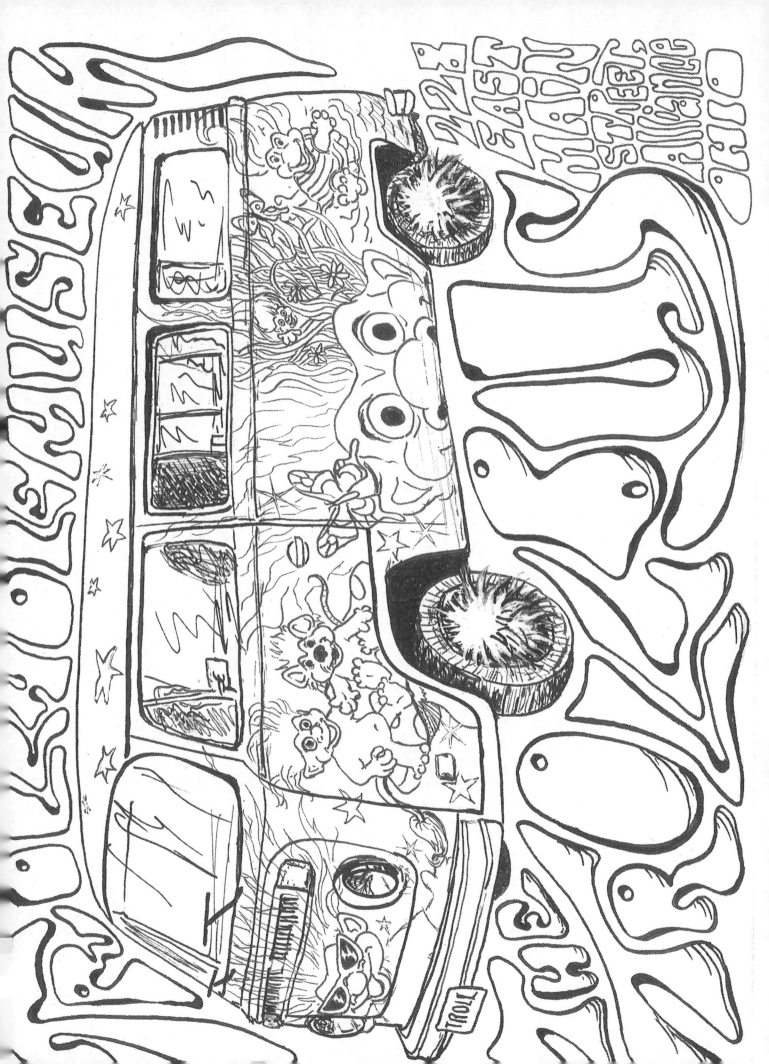

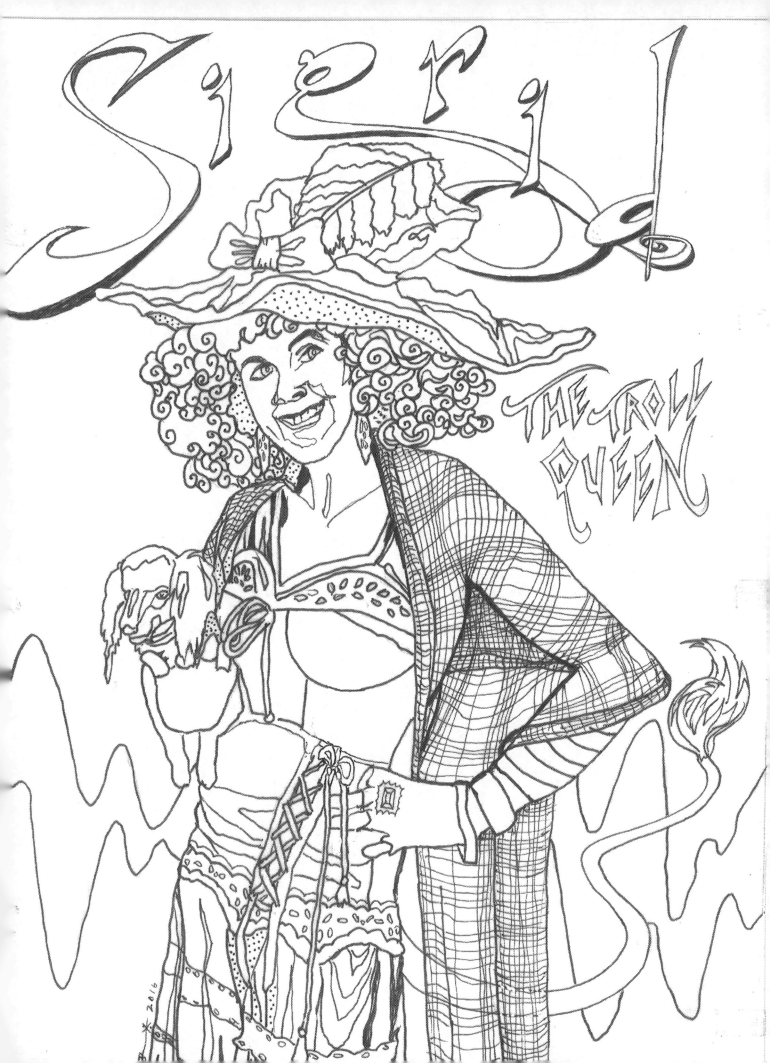

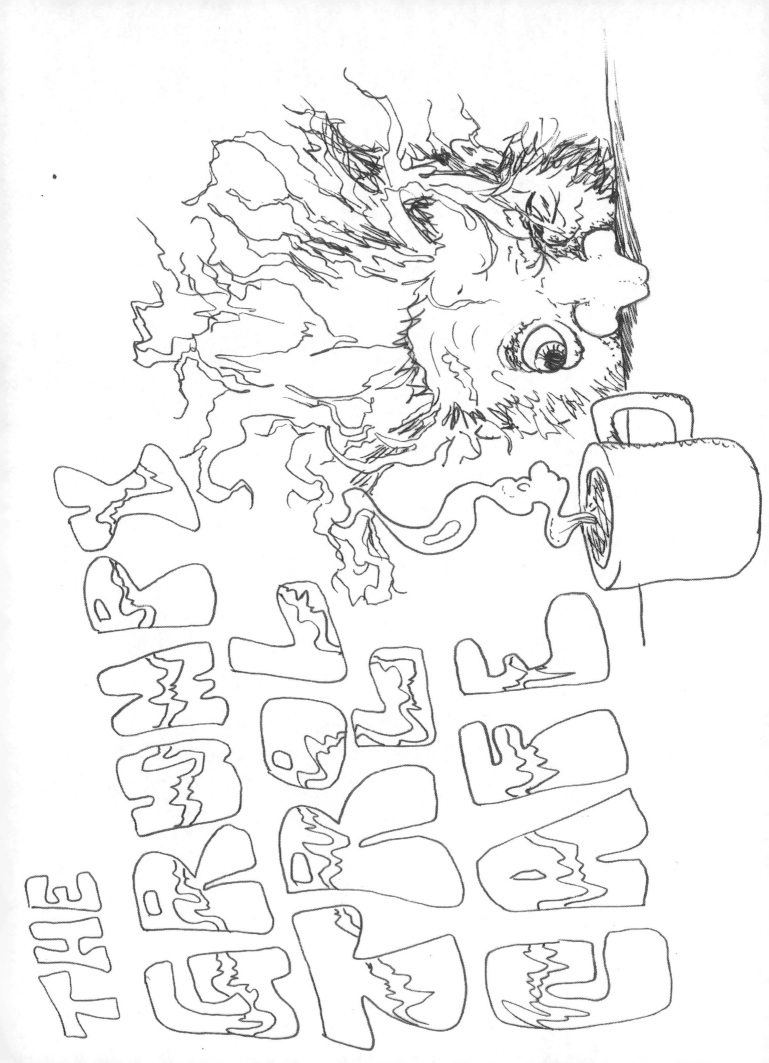

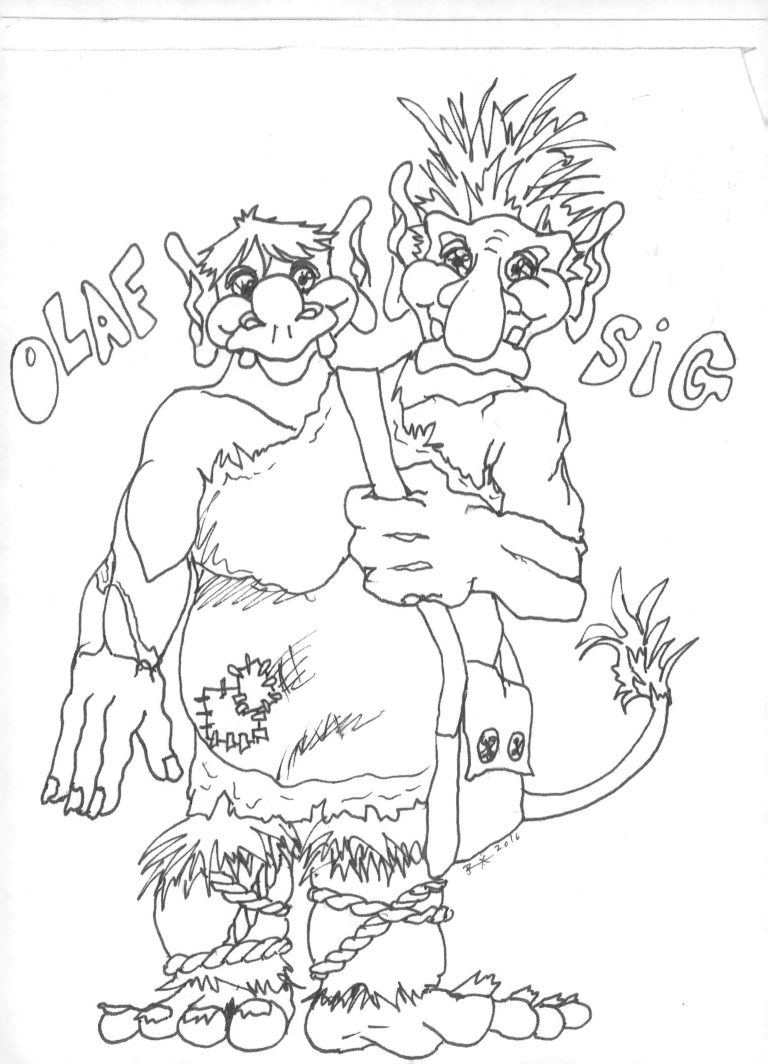

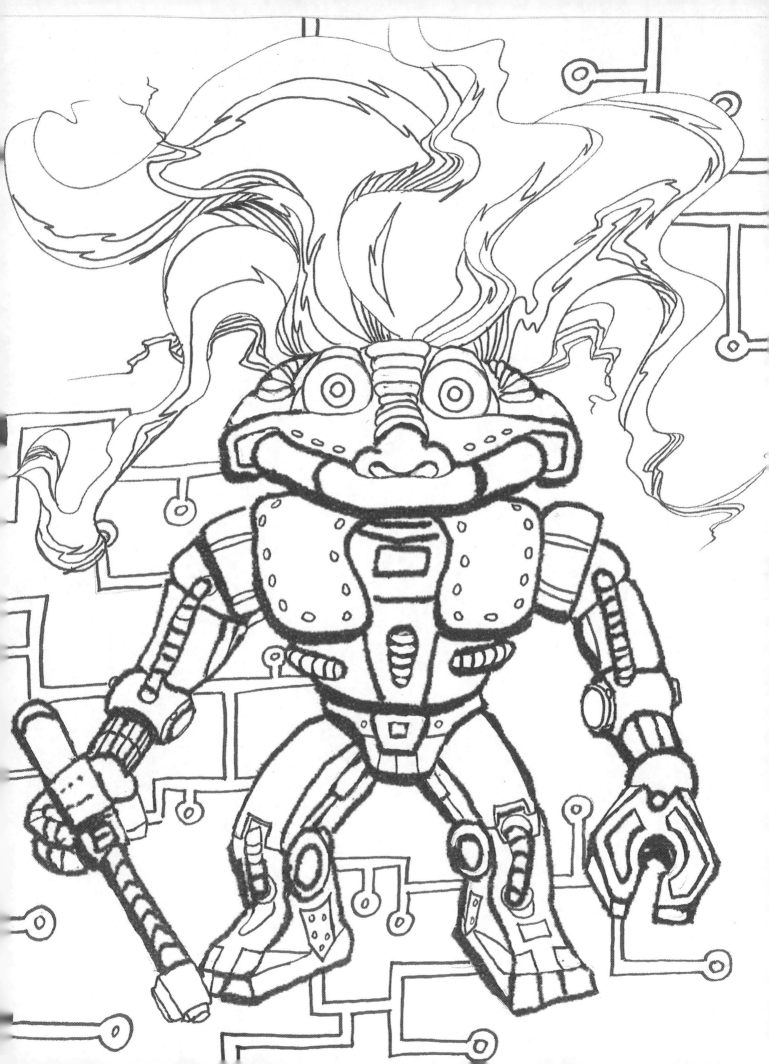

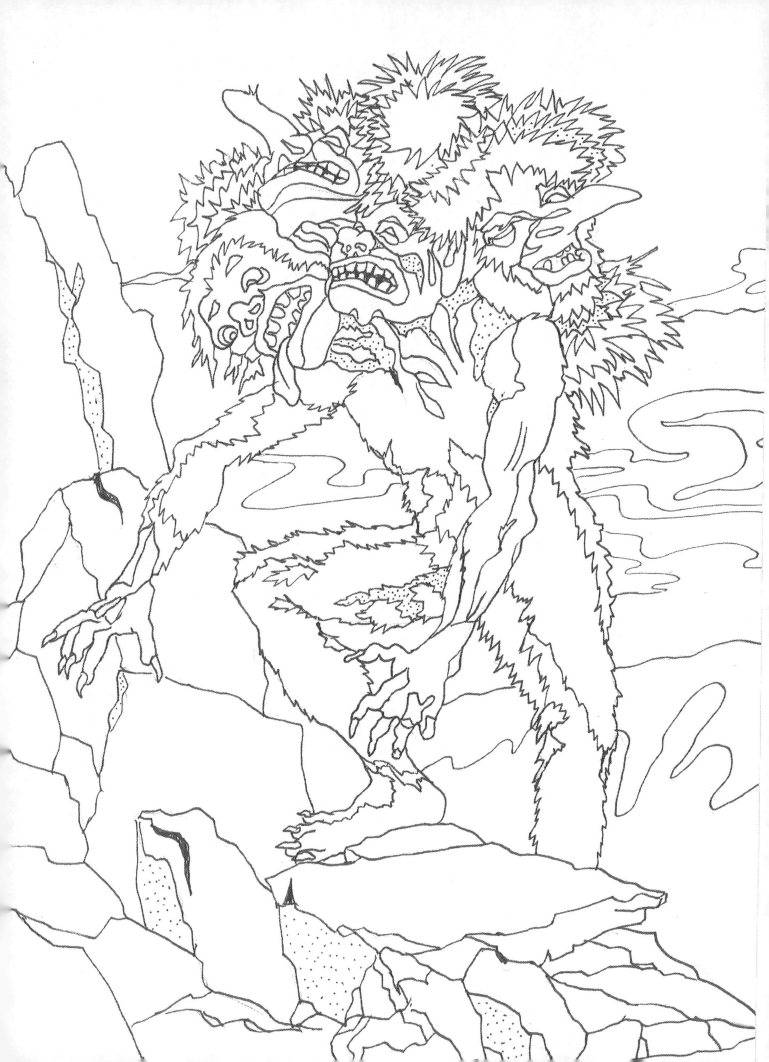

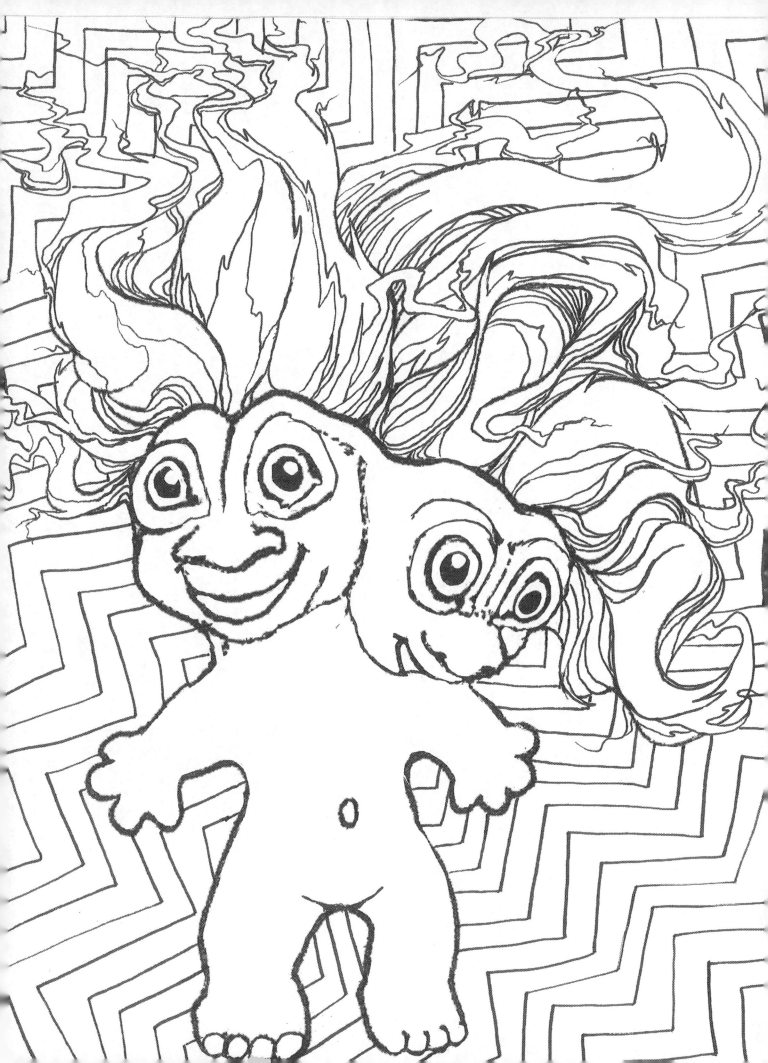

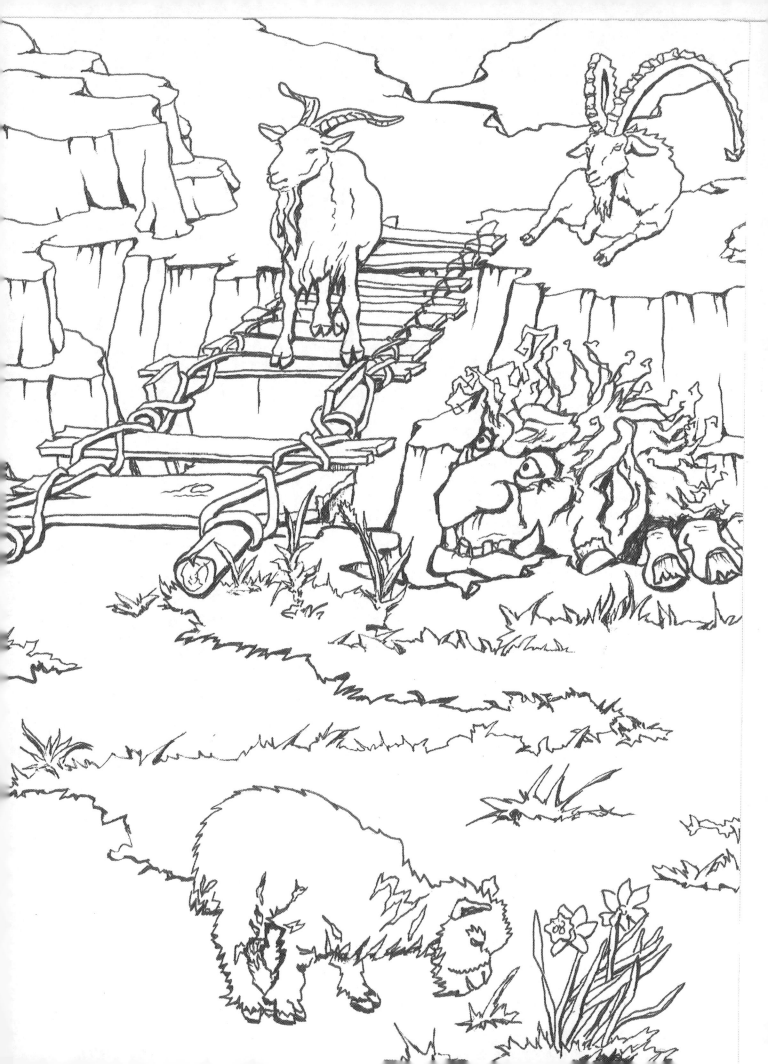

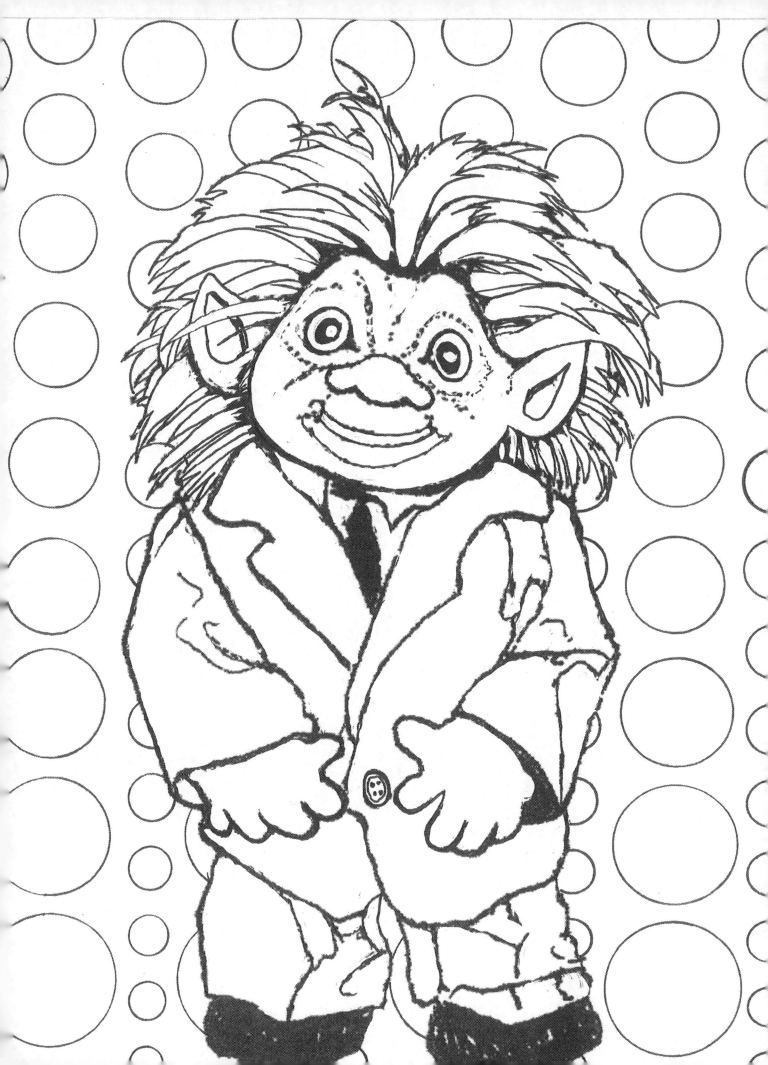

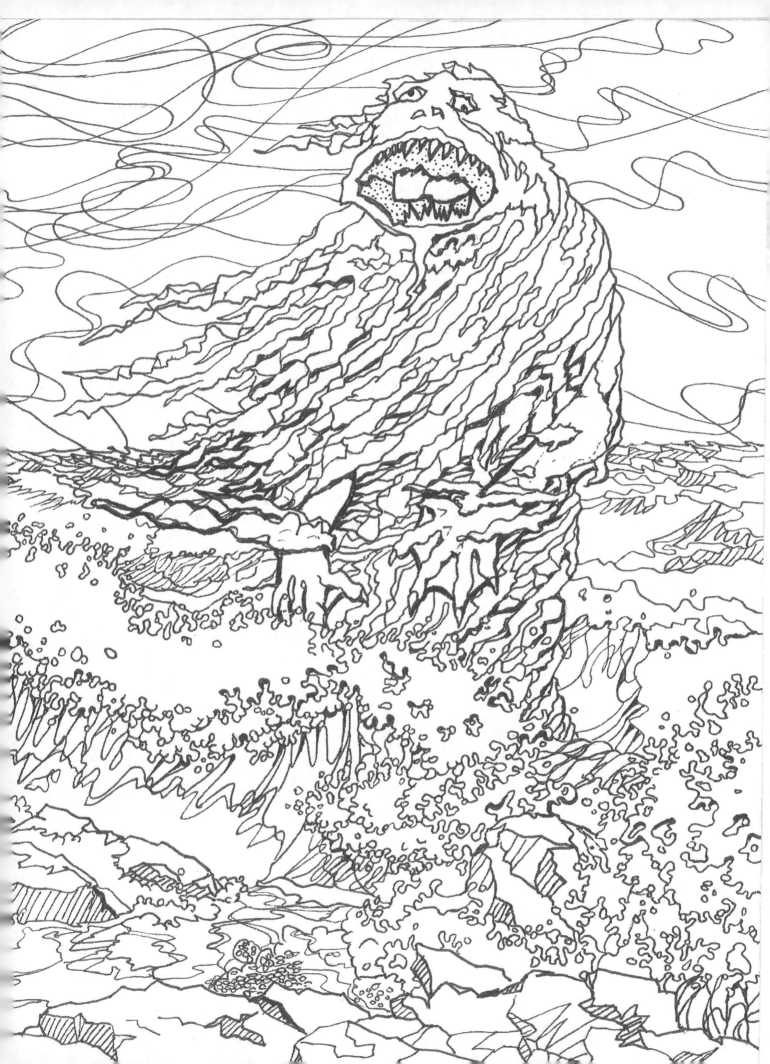

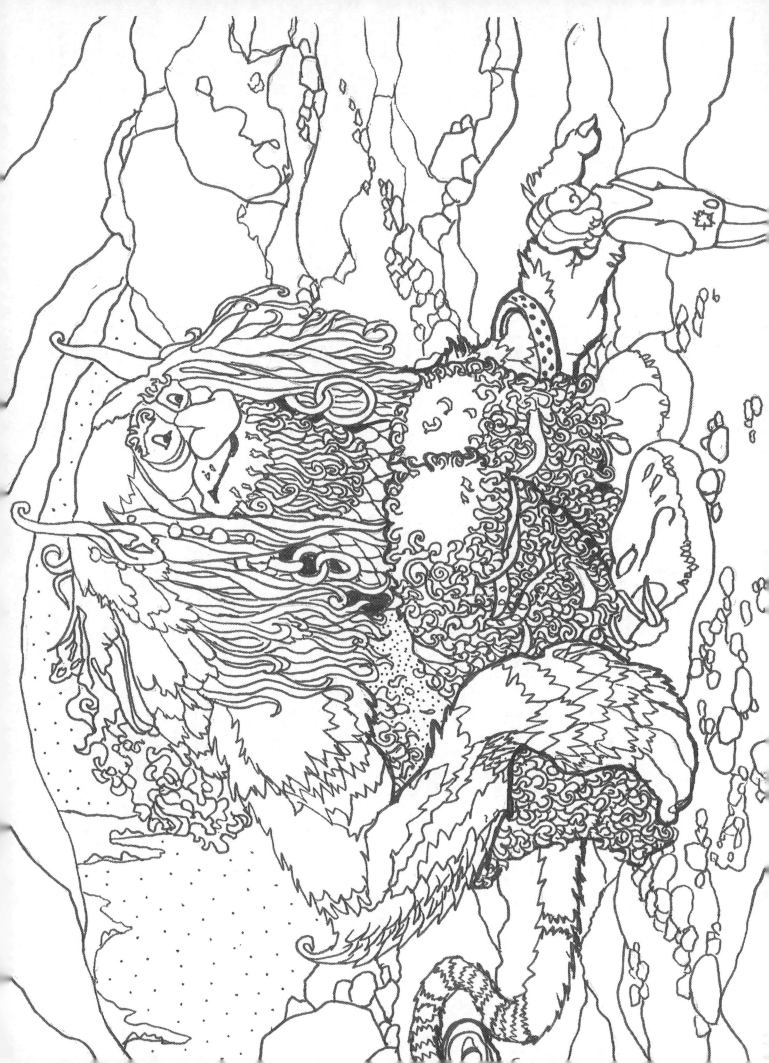

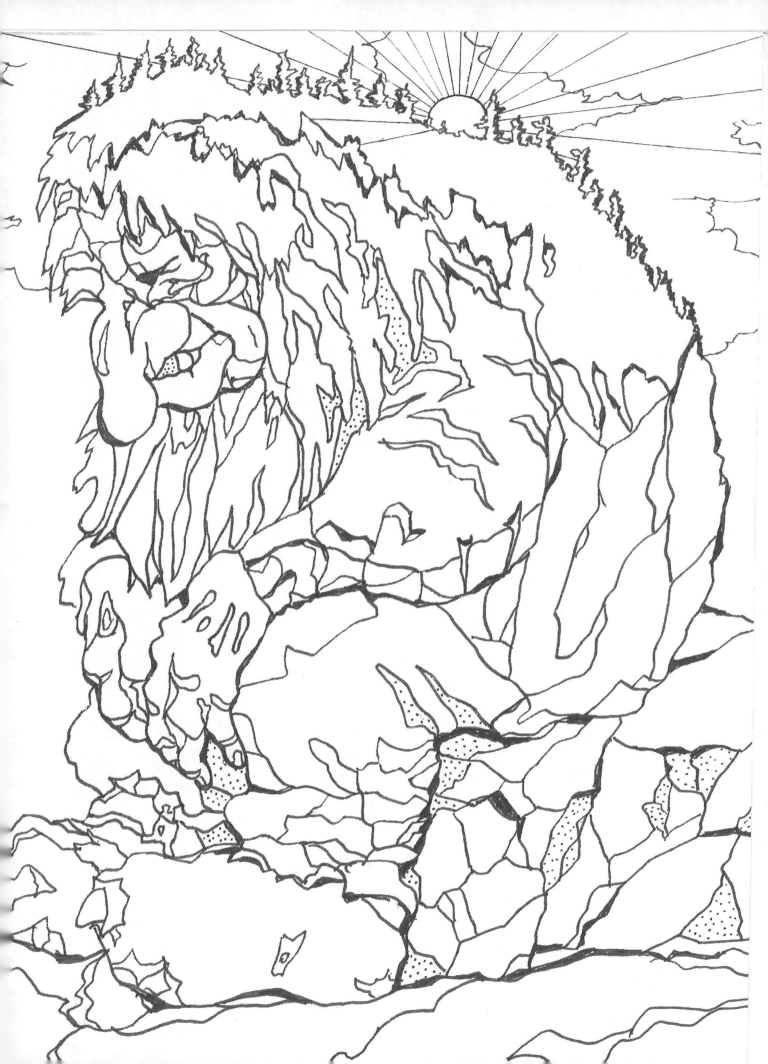

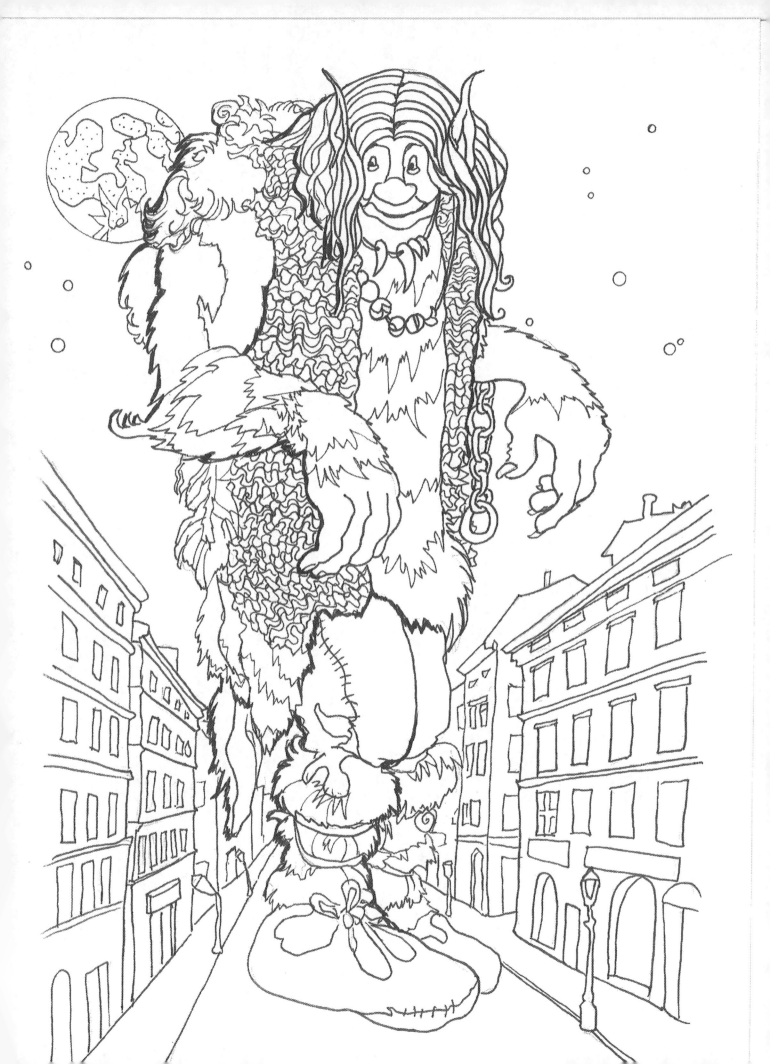

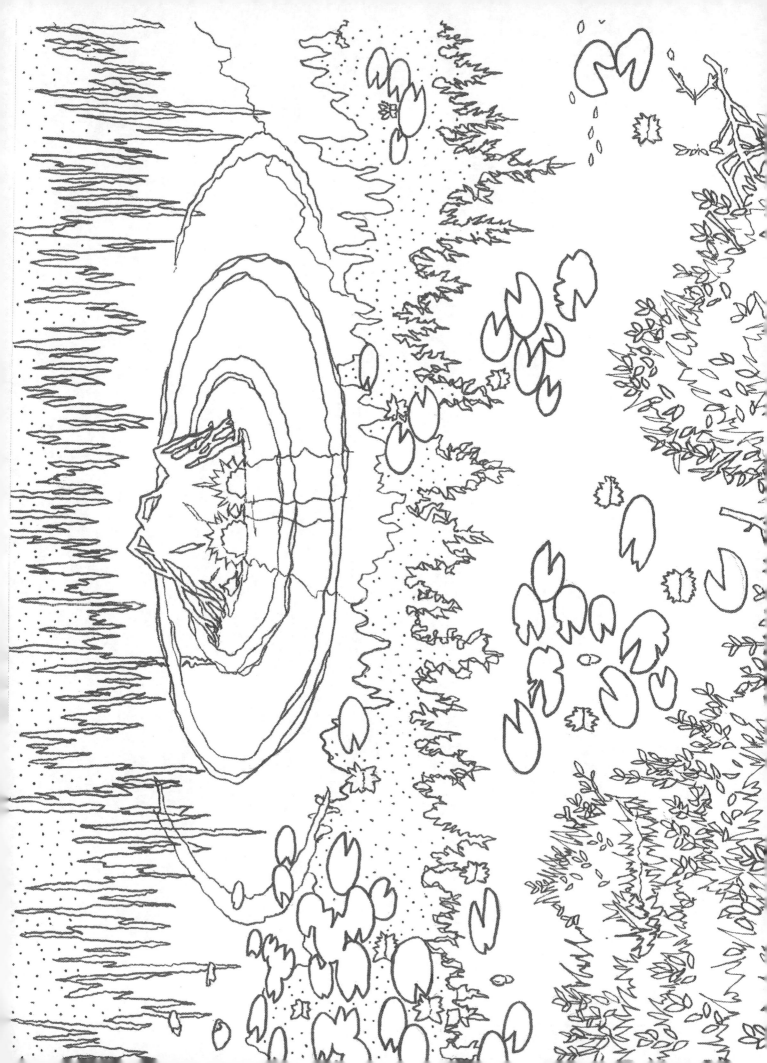

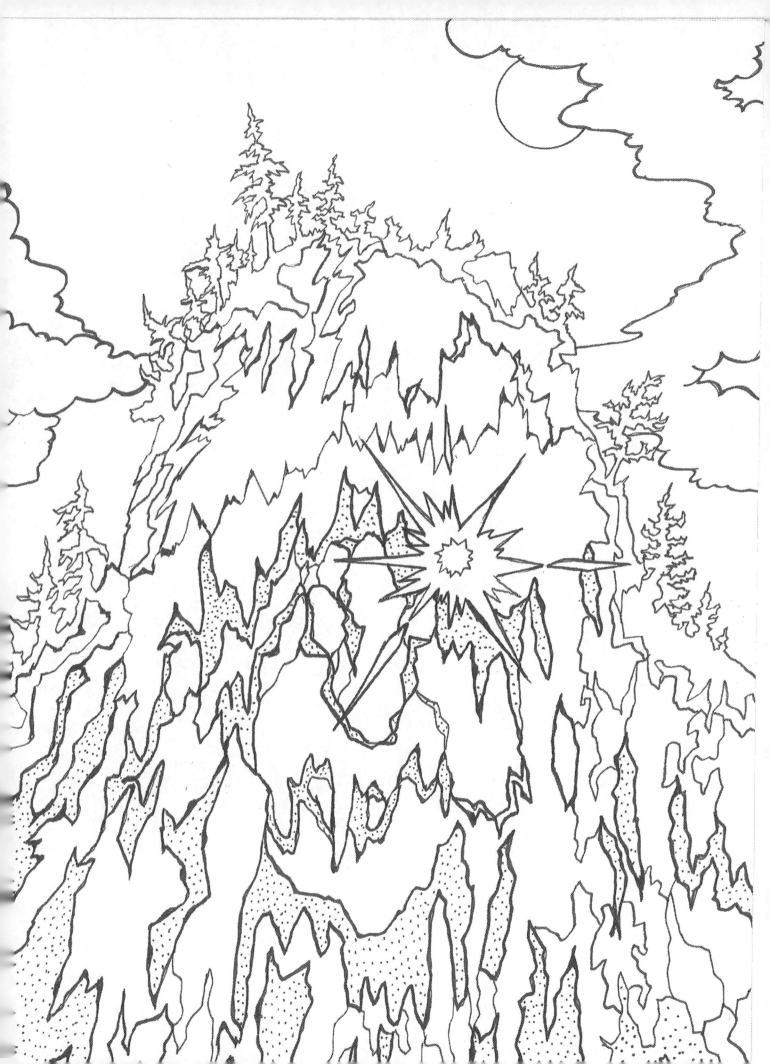

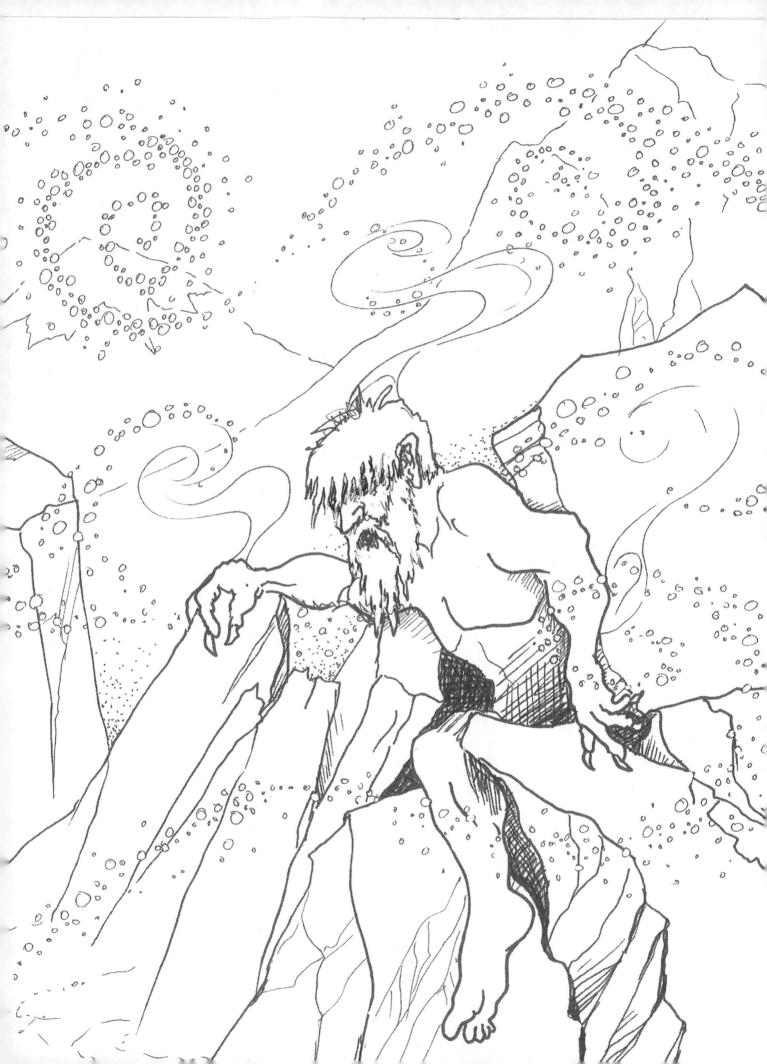

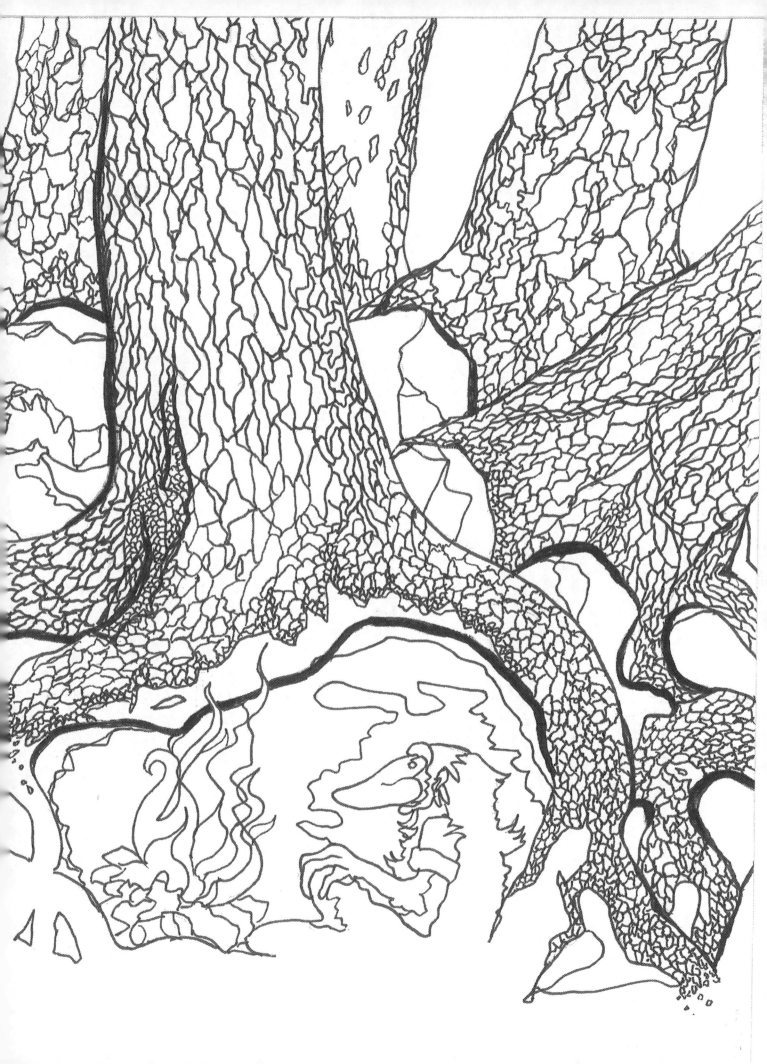

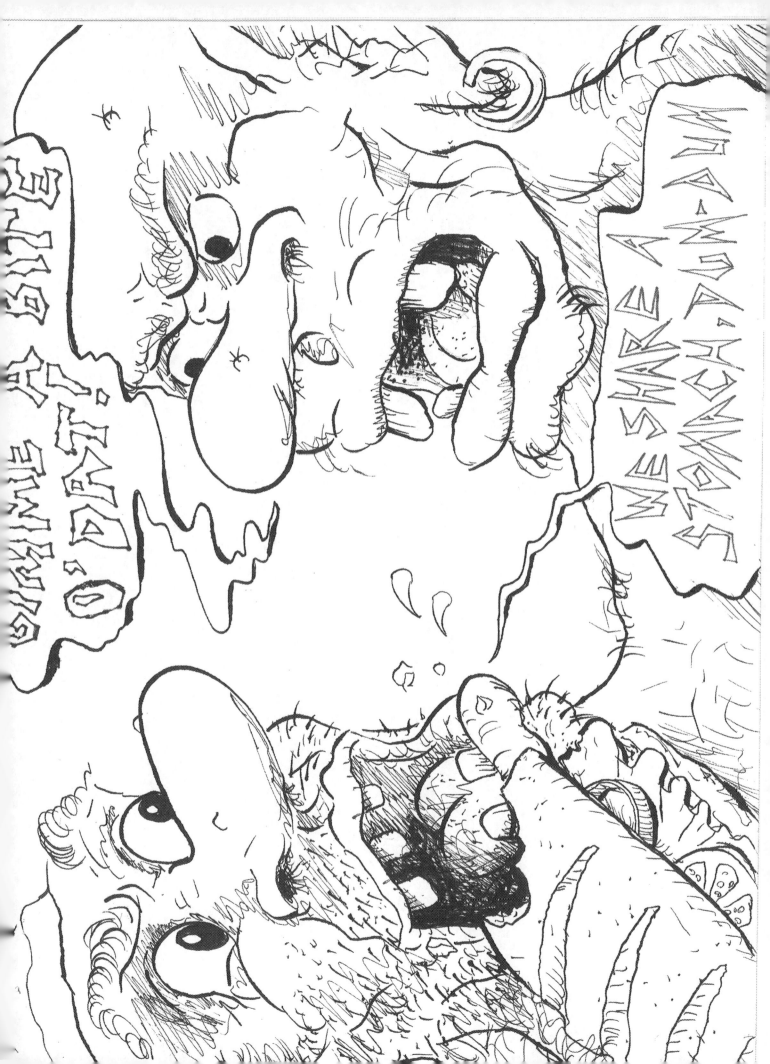

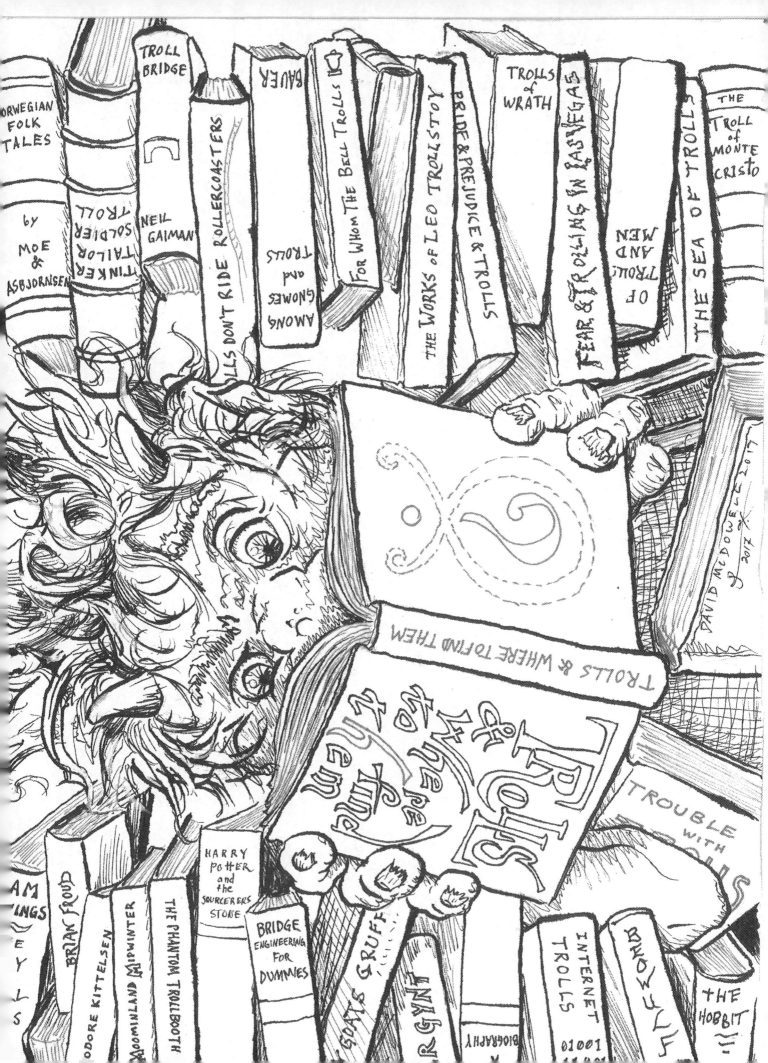

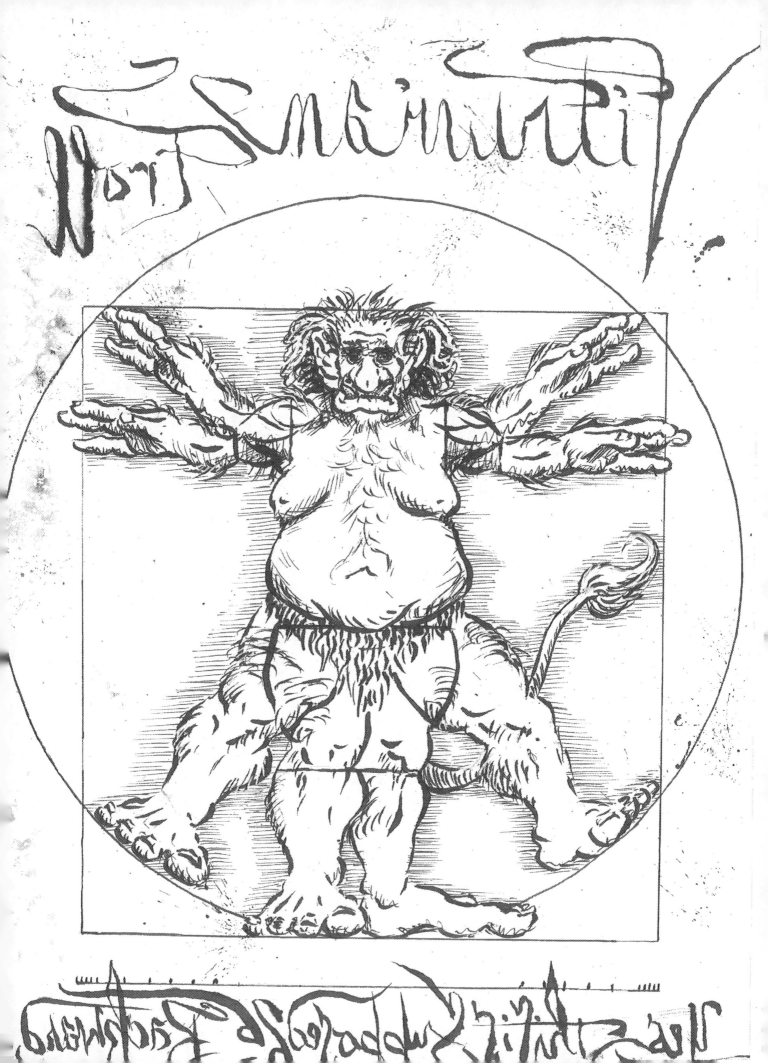

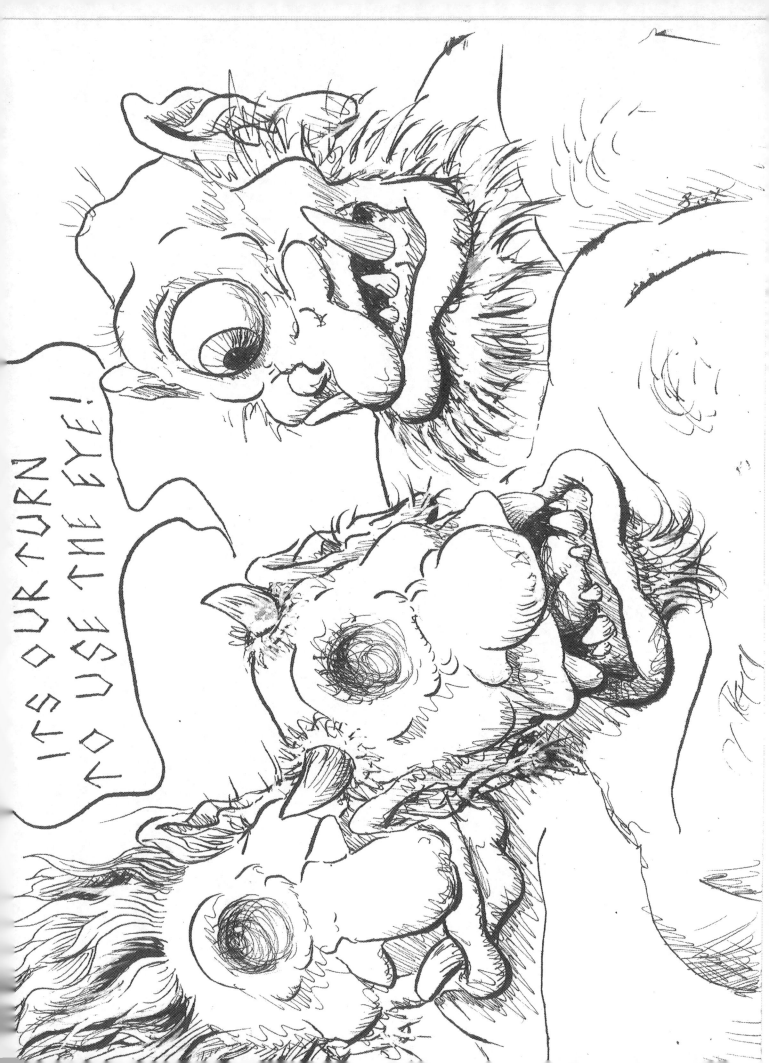

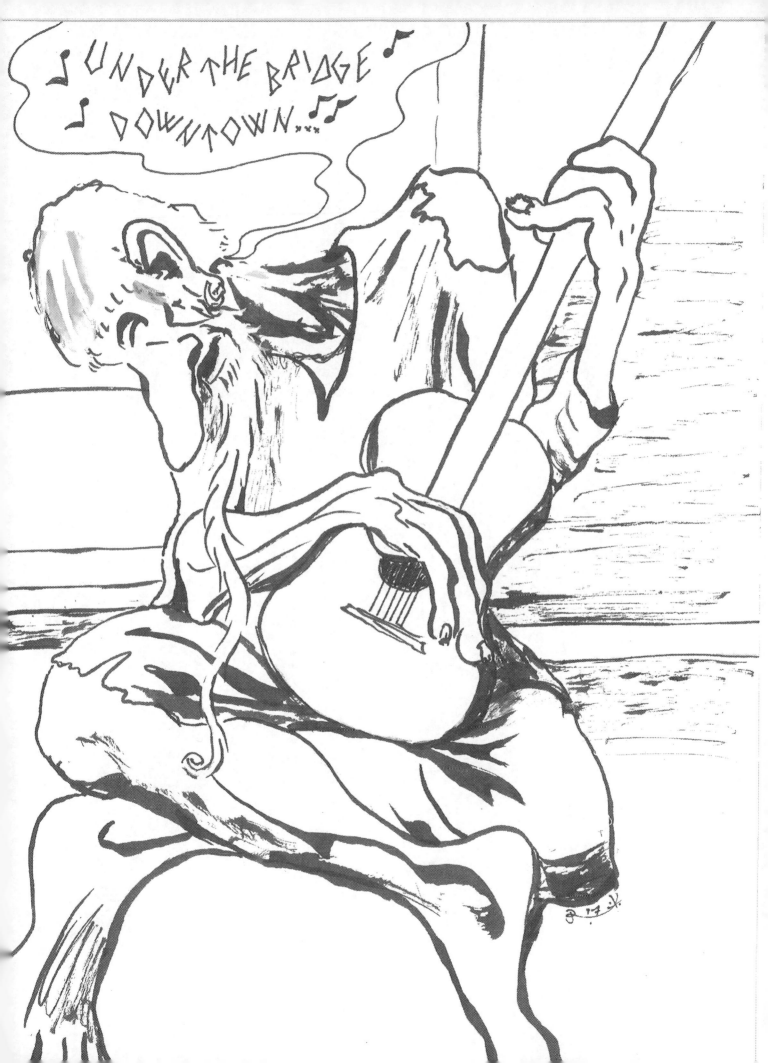

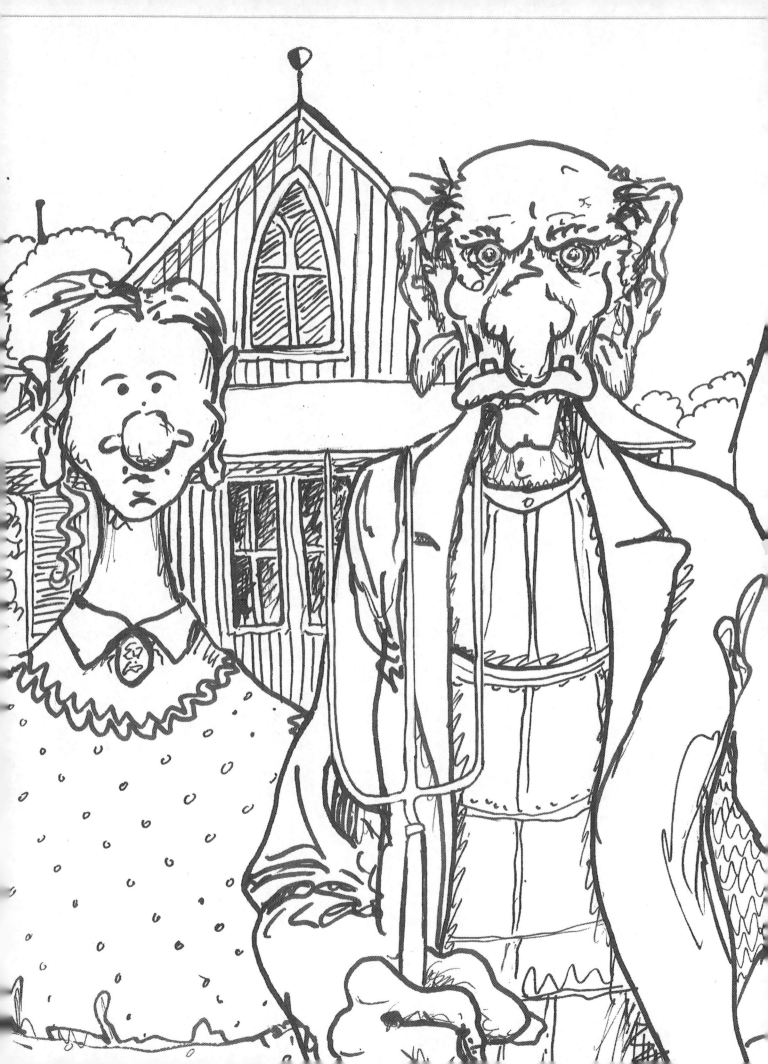

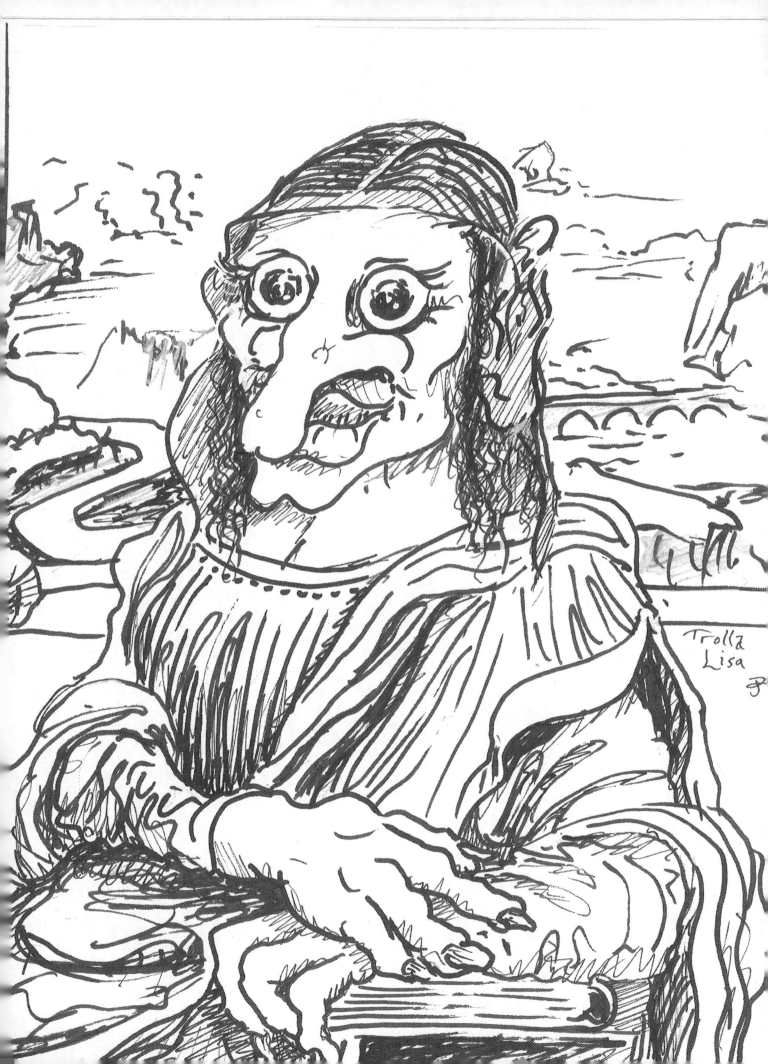

Trolla
Lisa

Coat of Arms of Vejen Denmark

1932   1977

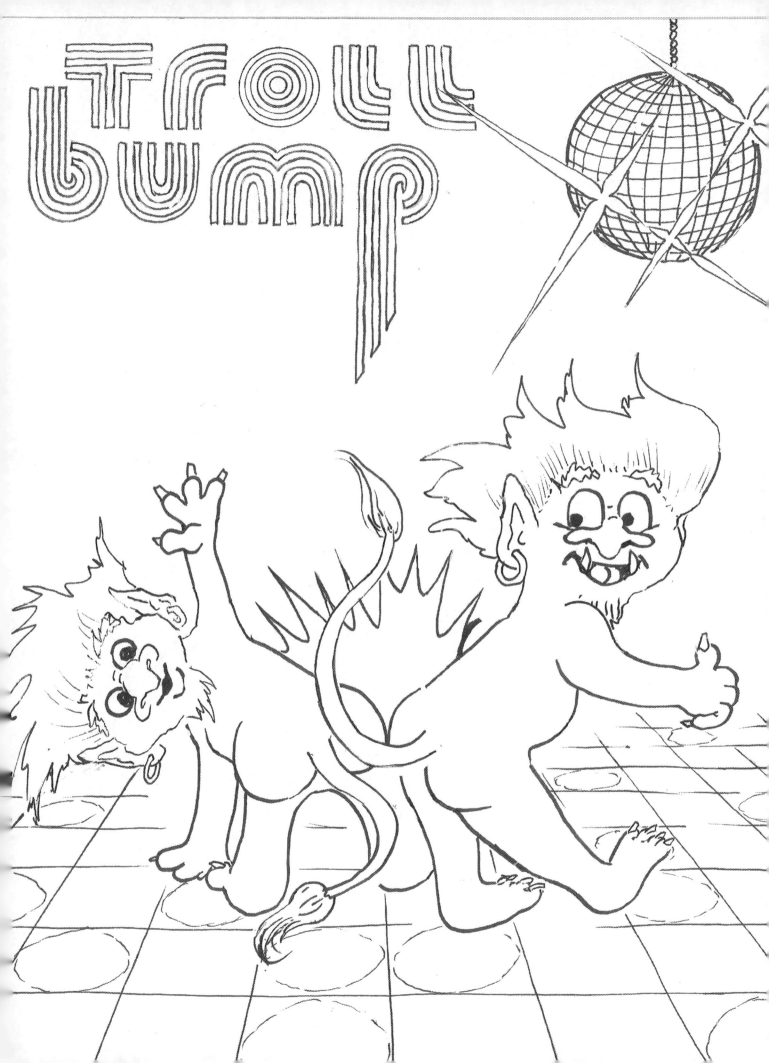

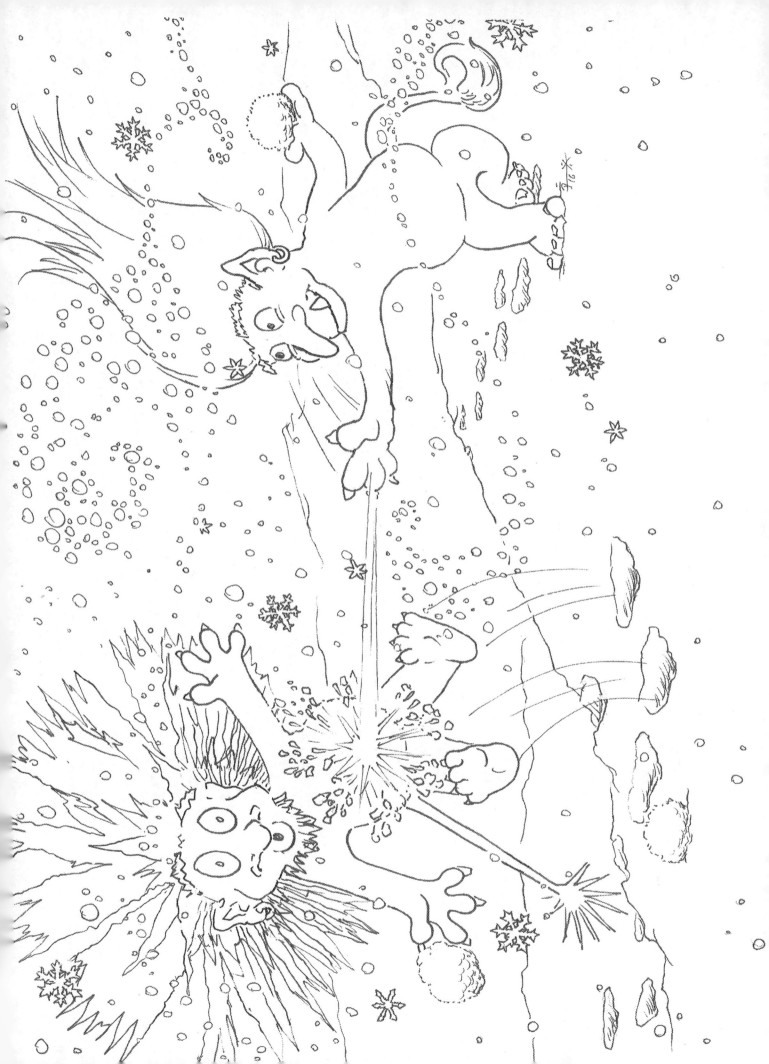

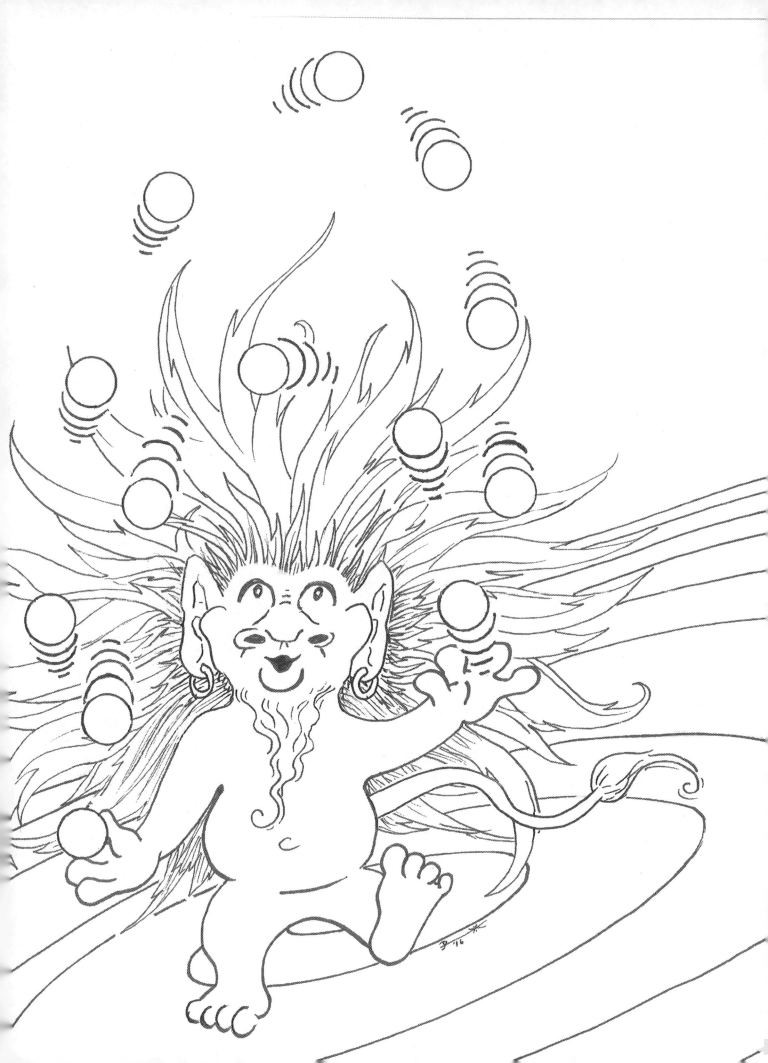

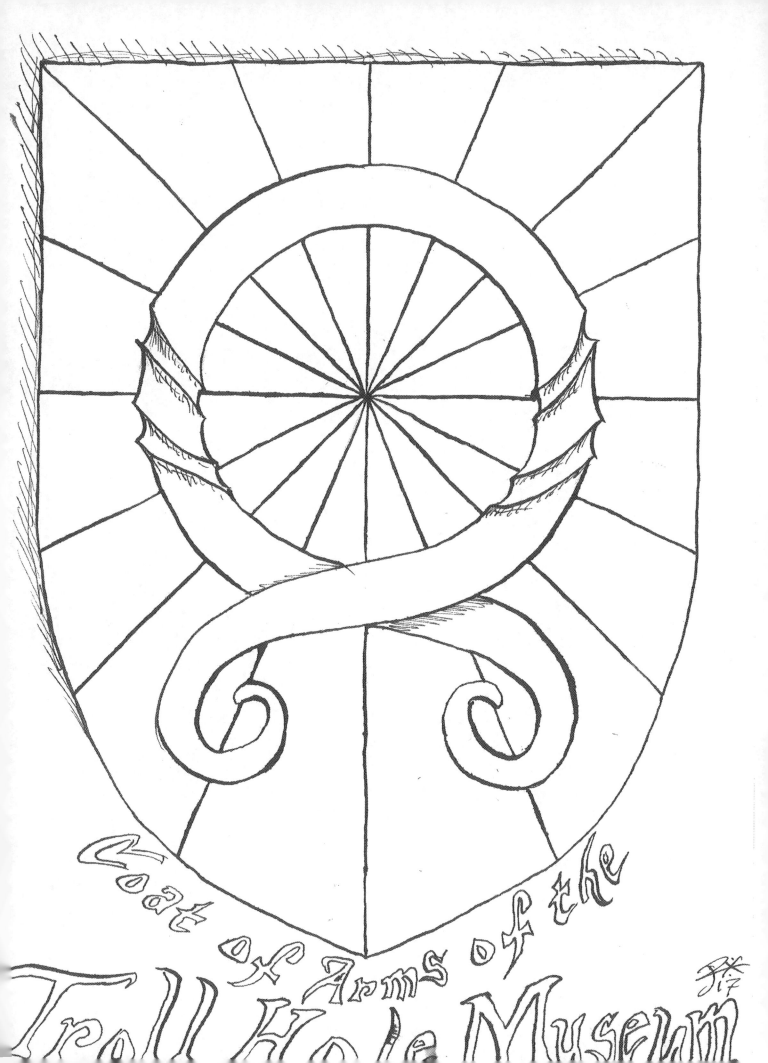

Coat of Arms of the
Troll Hole Museum

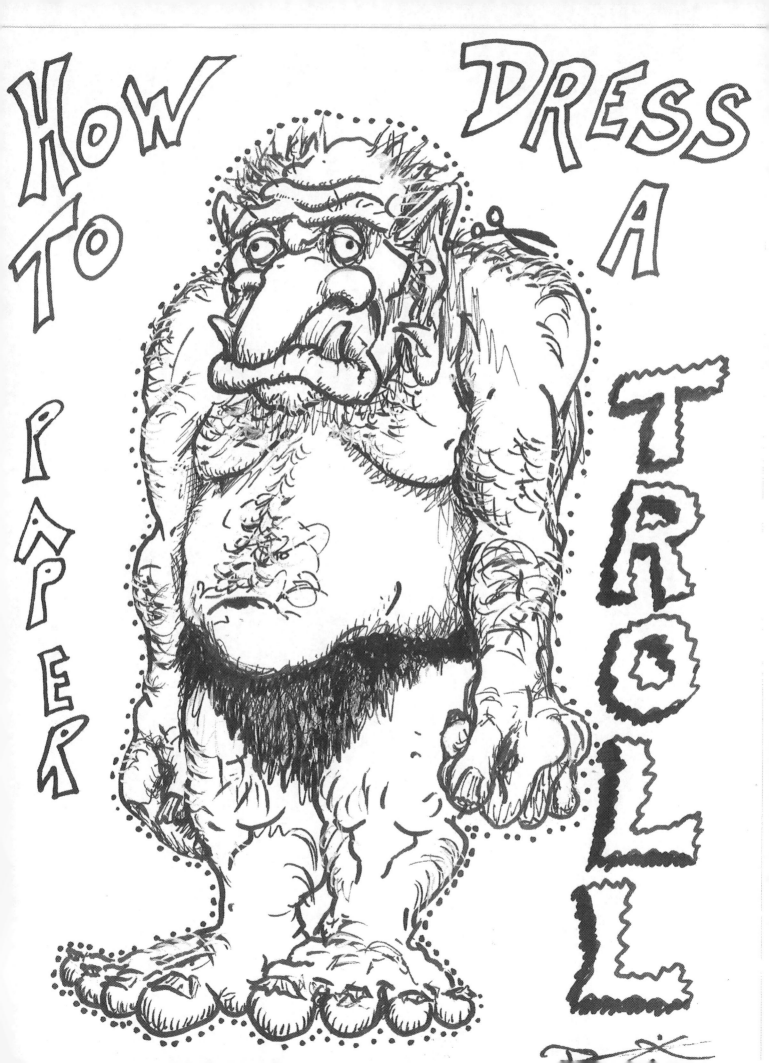

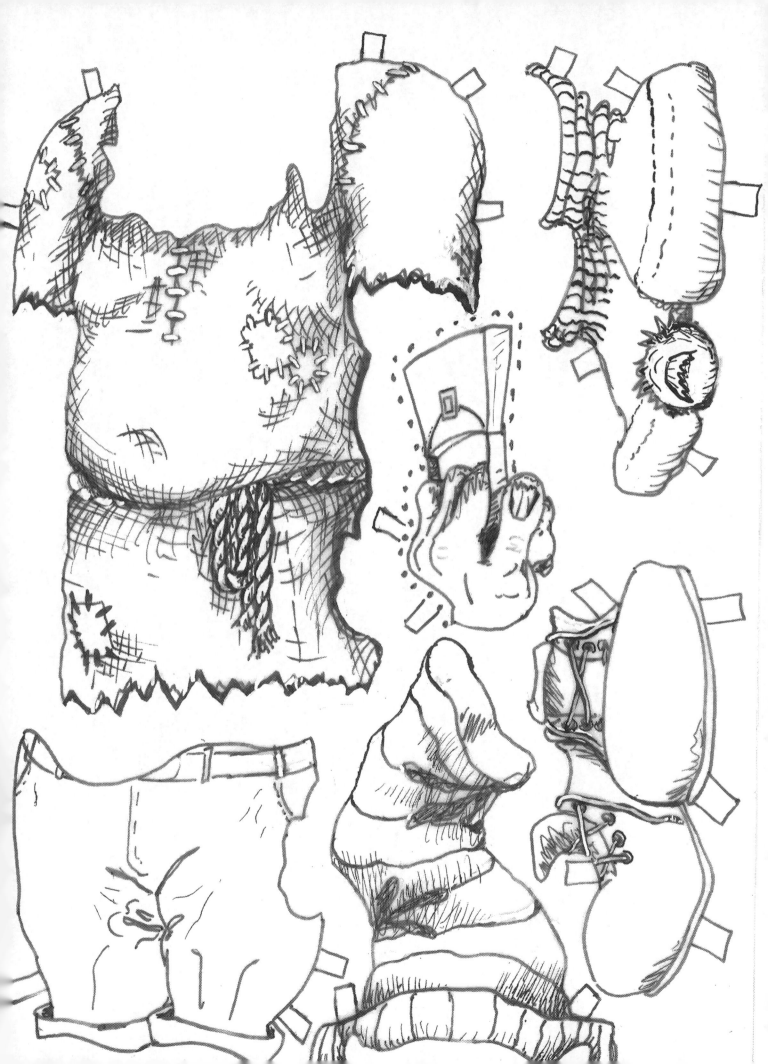

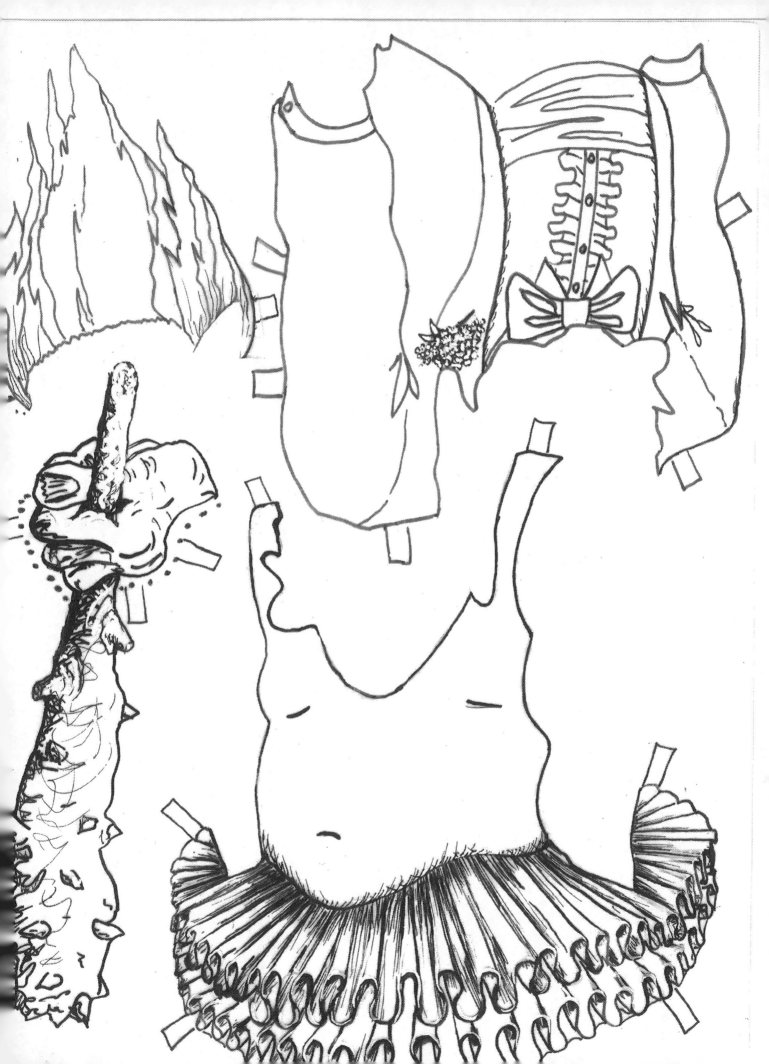

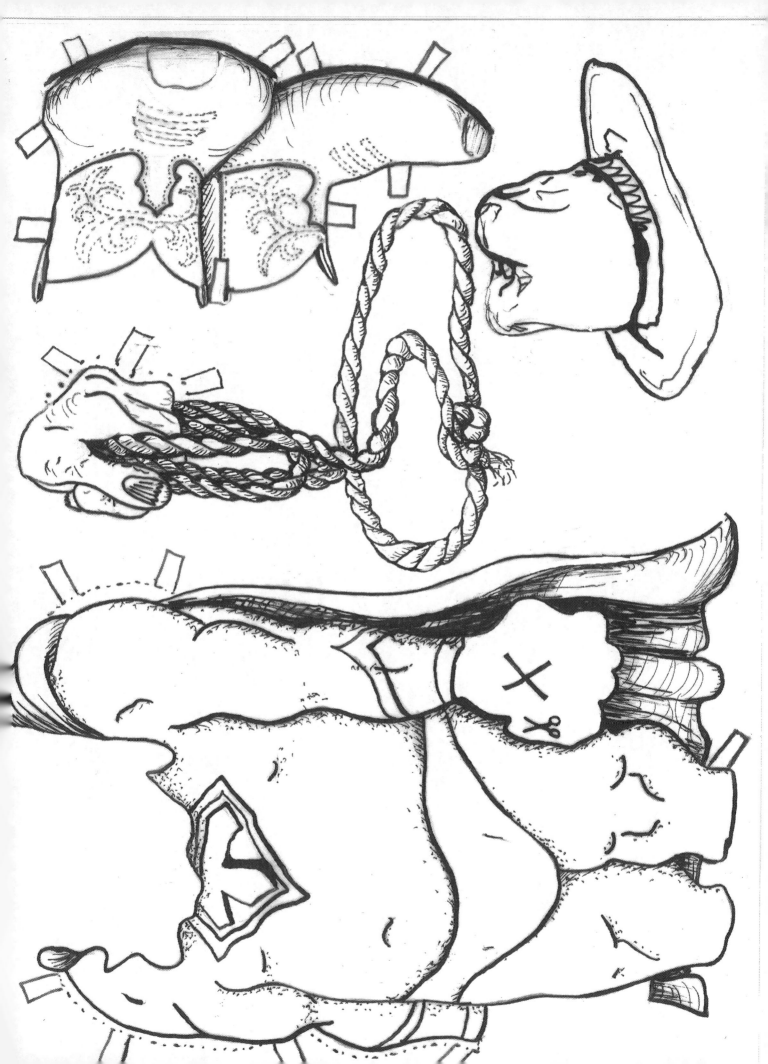

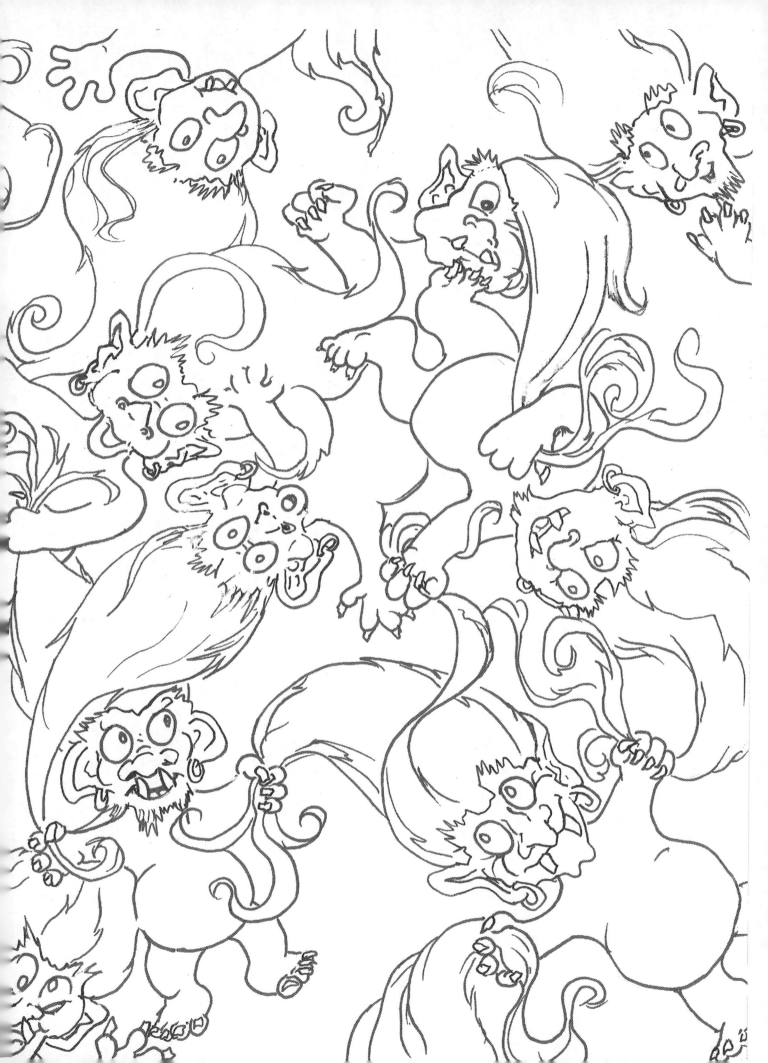

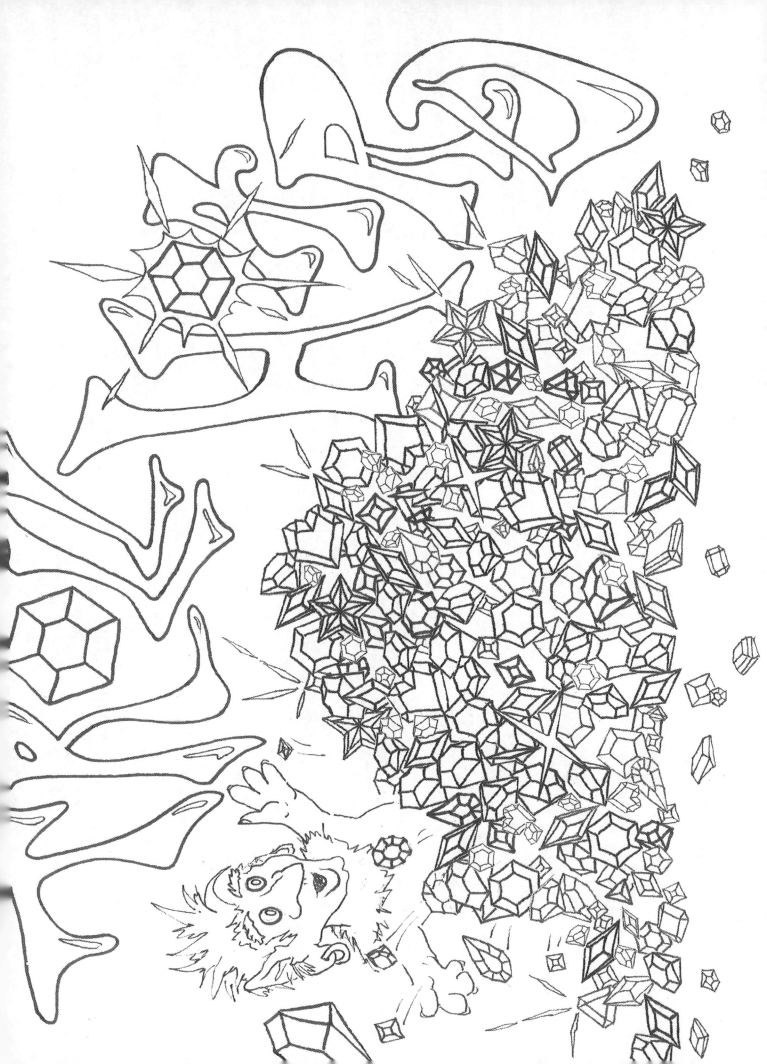

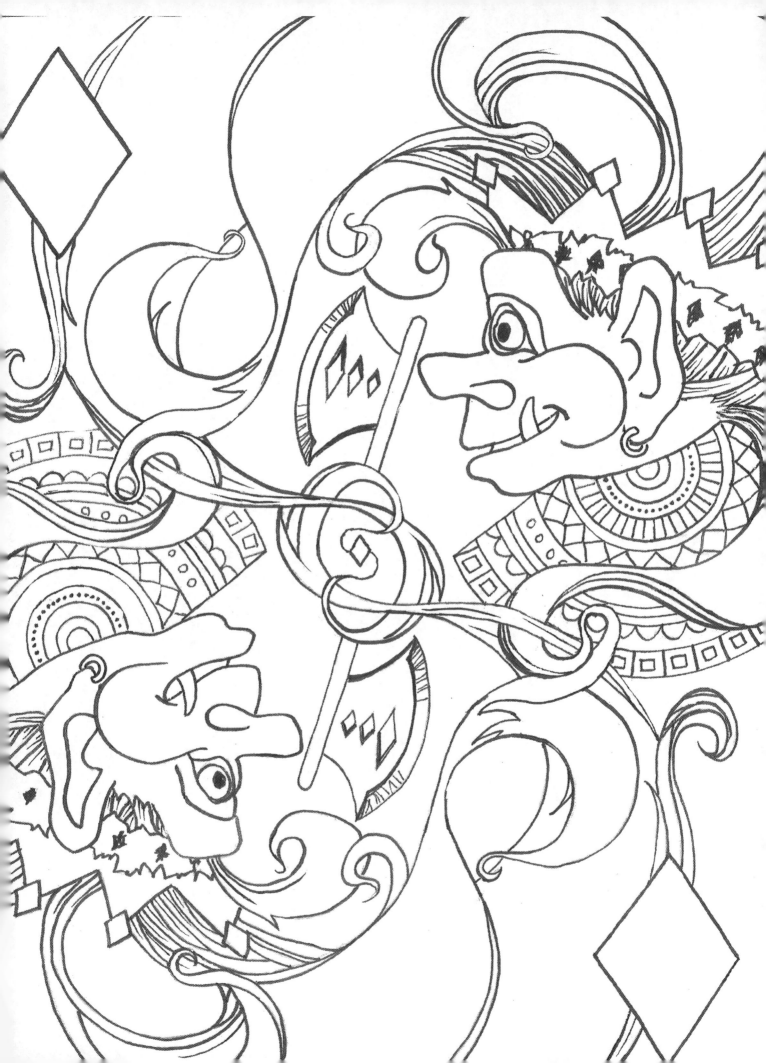

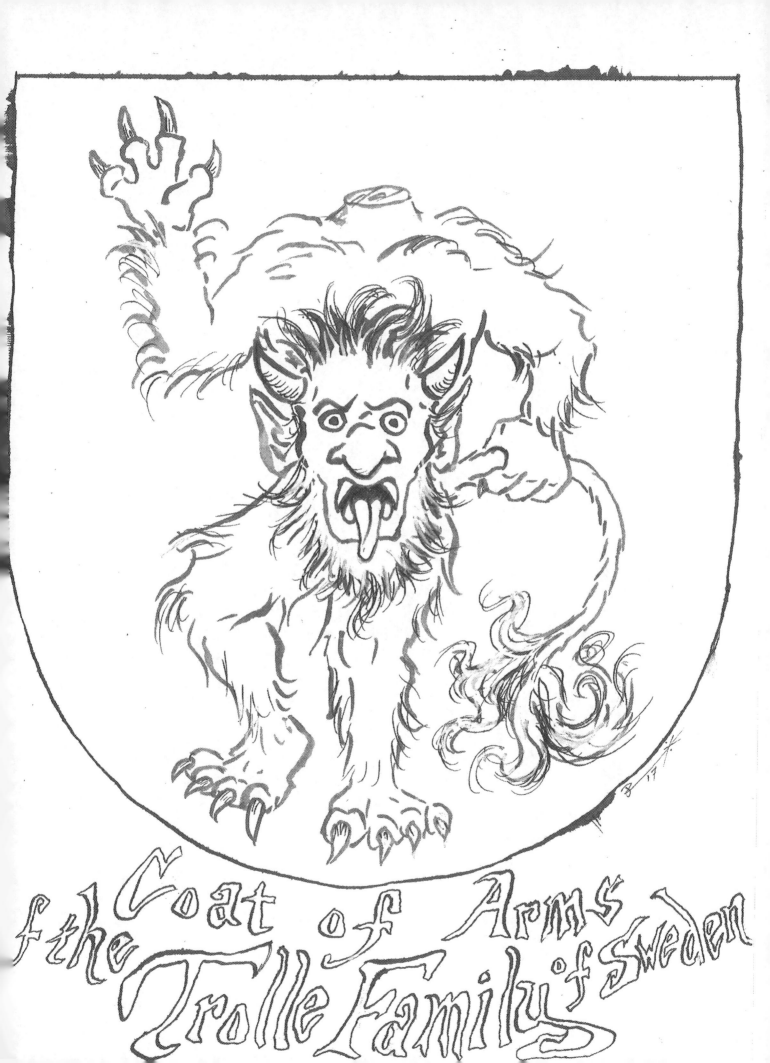

Coat of Arms of the Trolle Family of Sweden

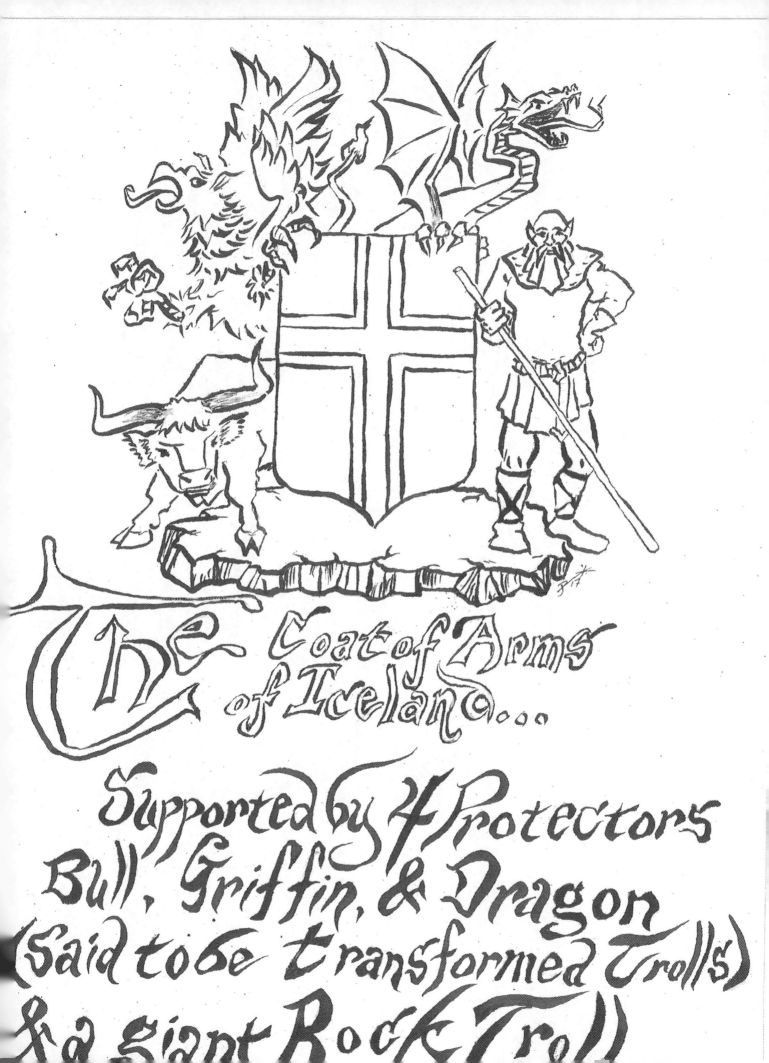

The Coat of Arms of Iceland...

Supported by 4 Protectors Bull, Griffin, & Dragon (said to be transformed Trolls) & a giant Rock Troll

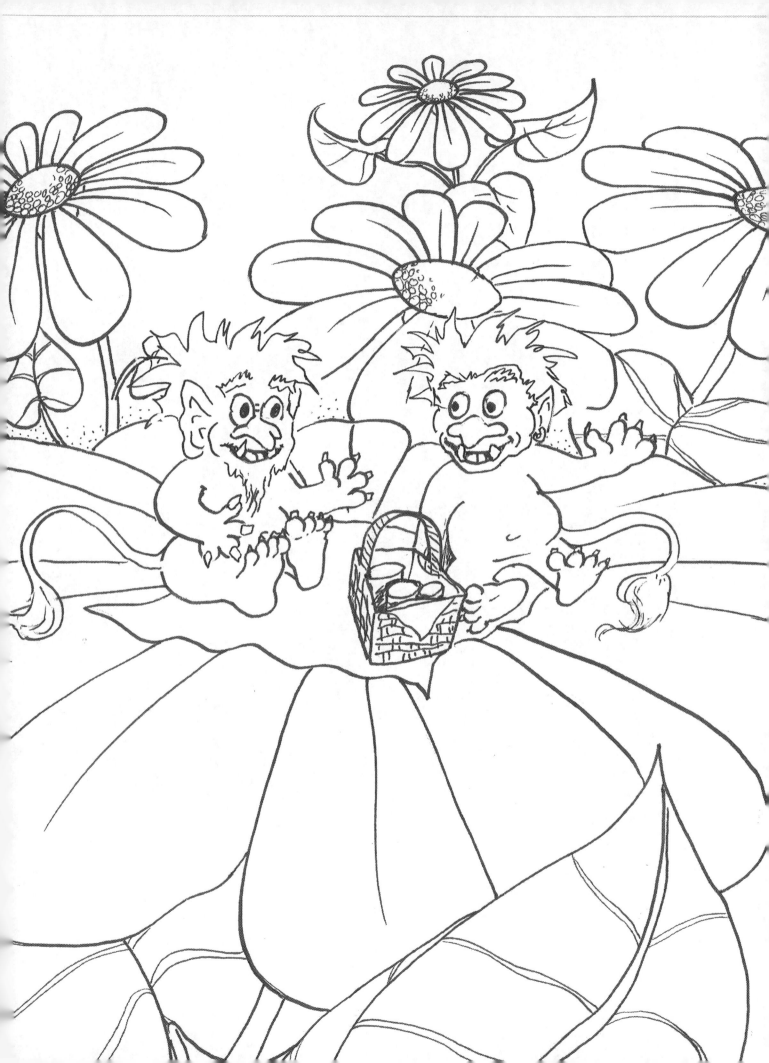

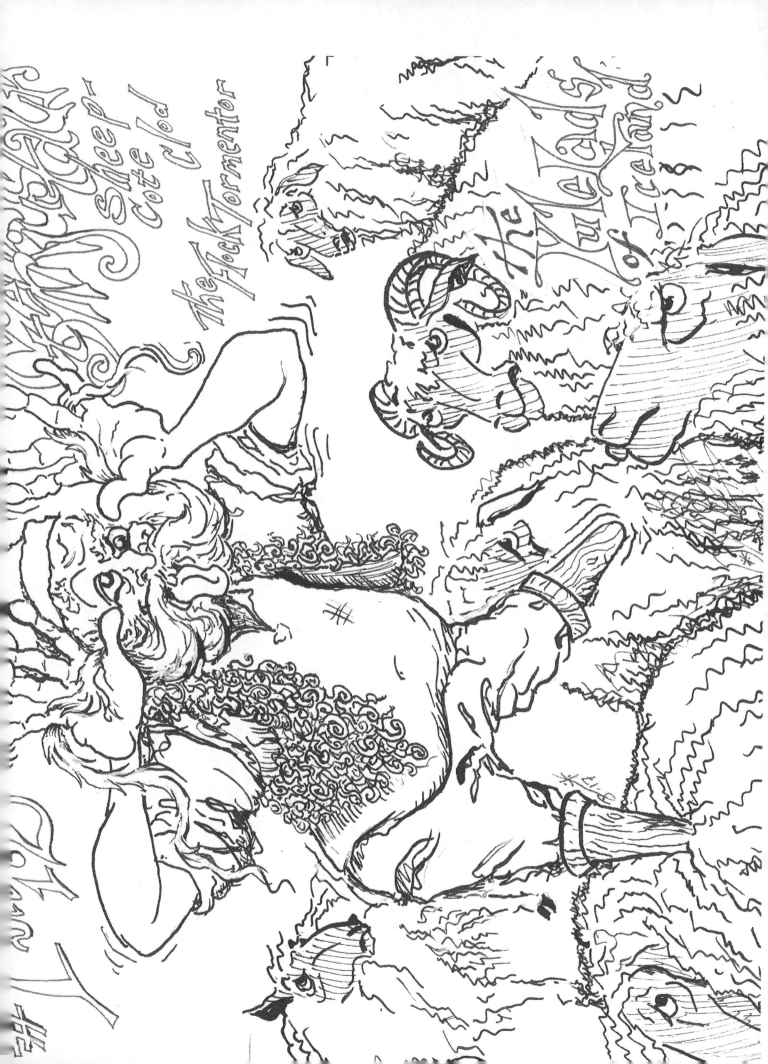

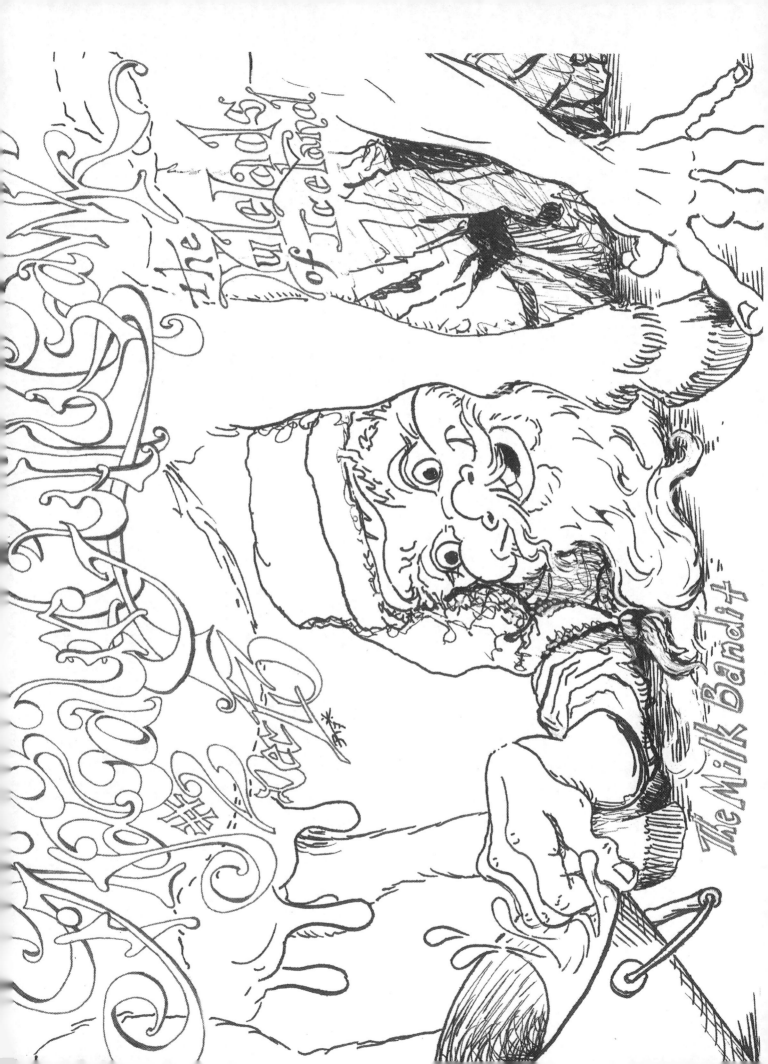

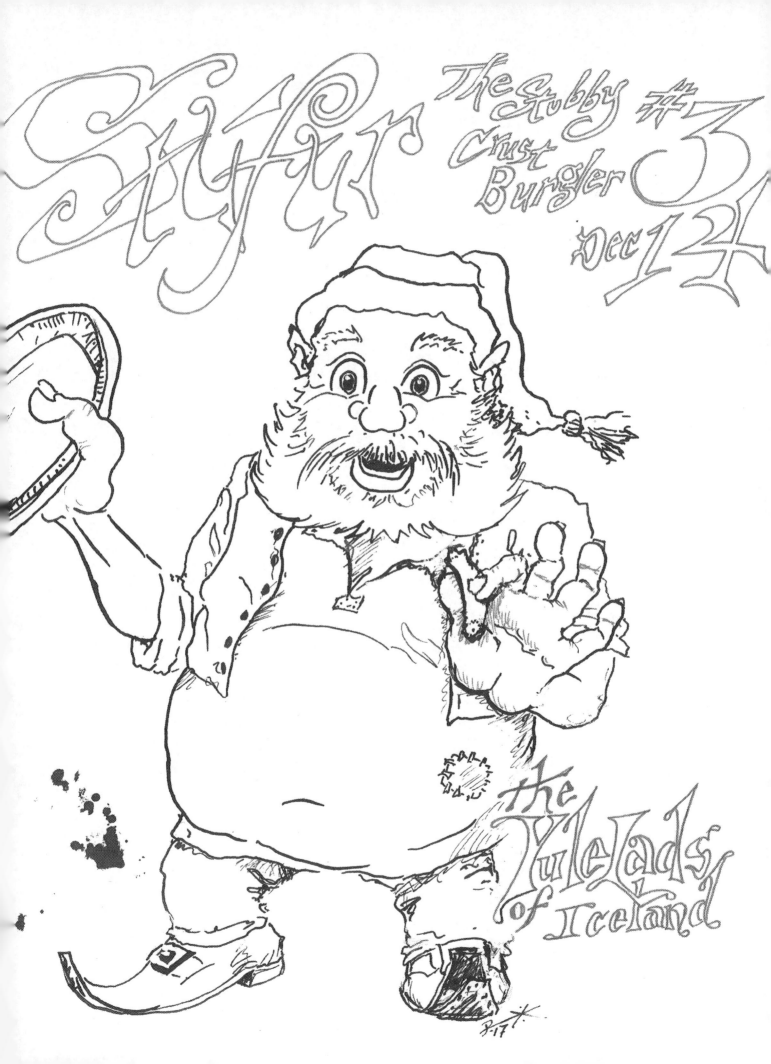

Stúfur The Stubby #3
Crust Burgler
Dec 12

The YuleLads of Iceland

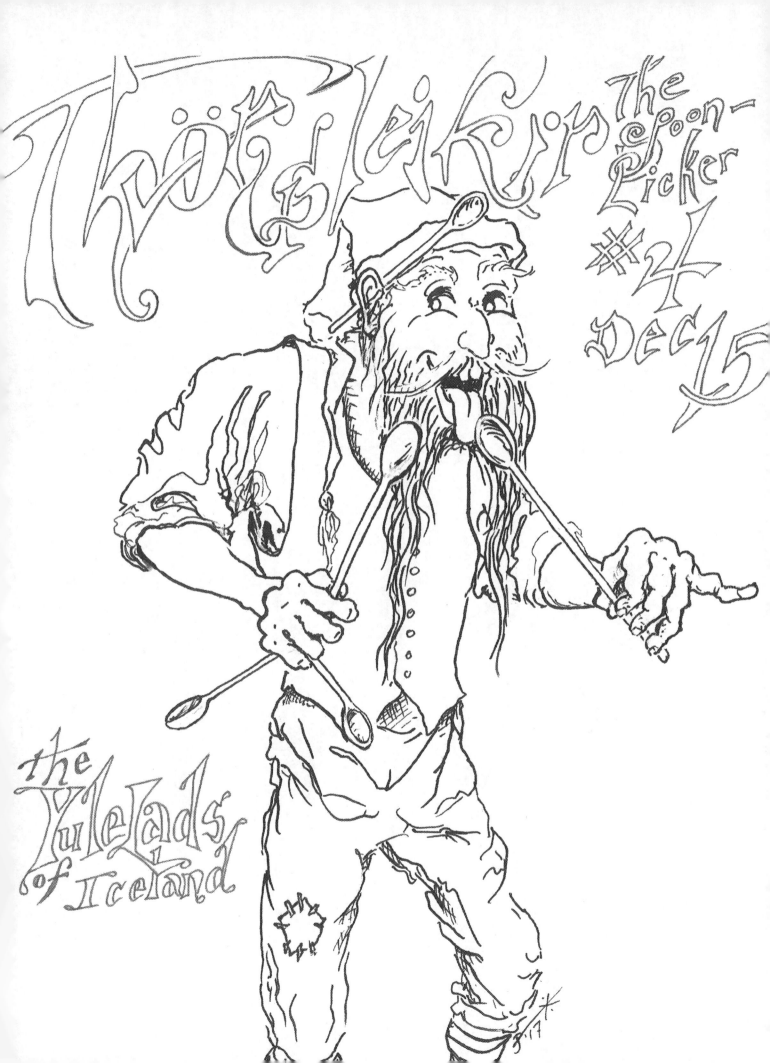

Thröstleikur: The Spoon-Picker #2 Dec 15

the Yule Lads of Iceland

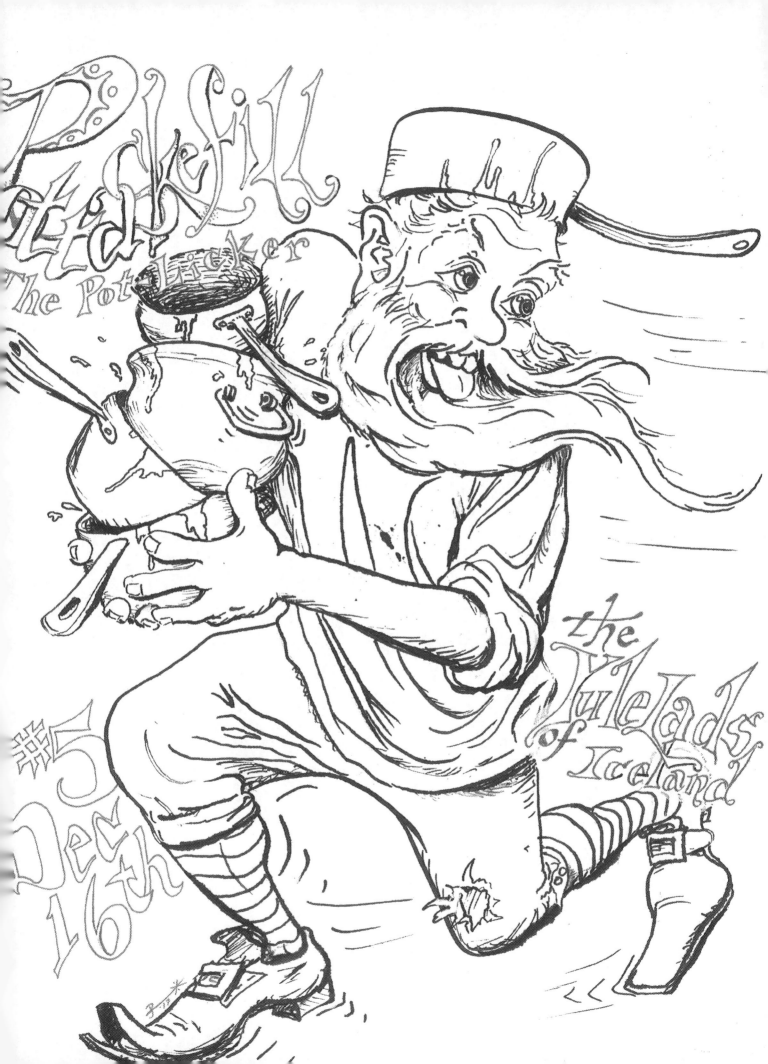

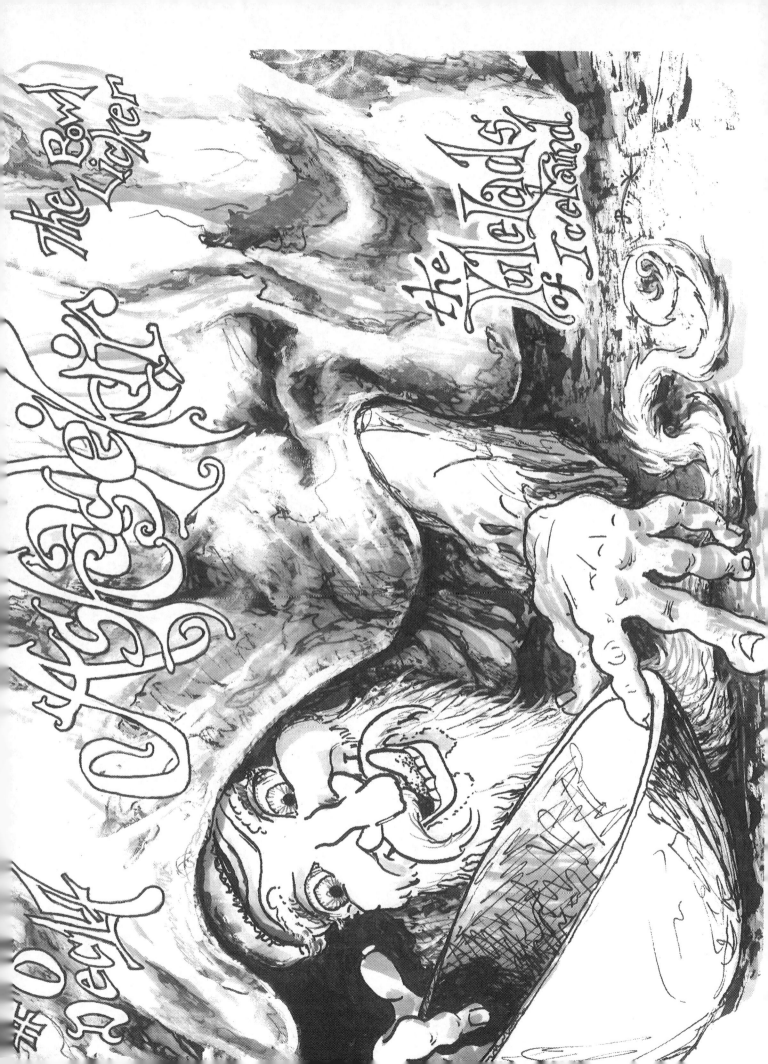

The Bowl Licker

The Yuletads of Iceland

Askasleikir

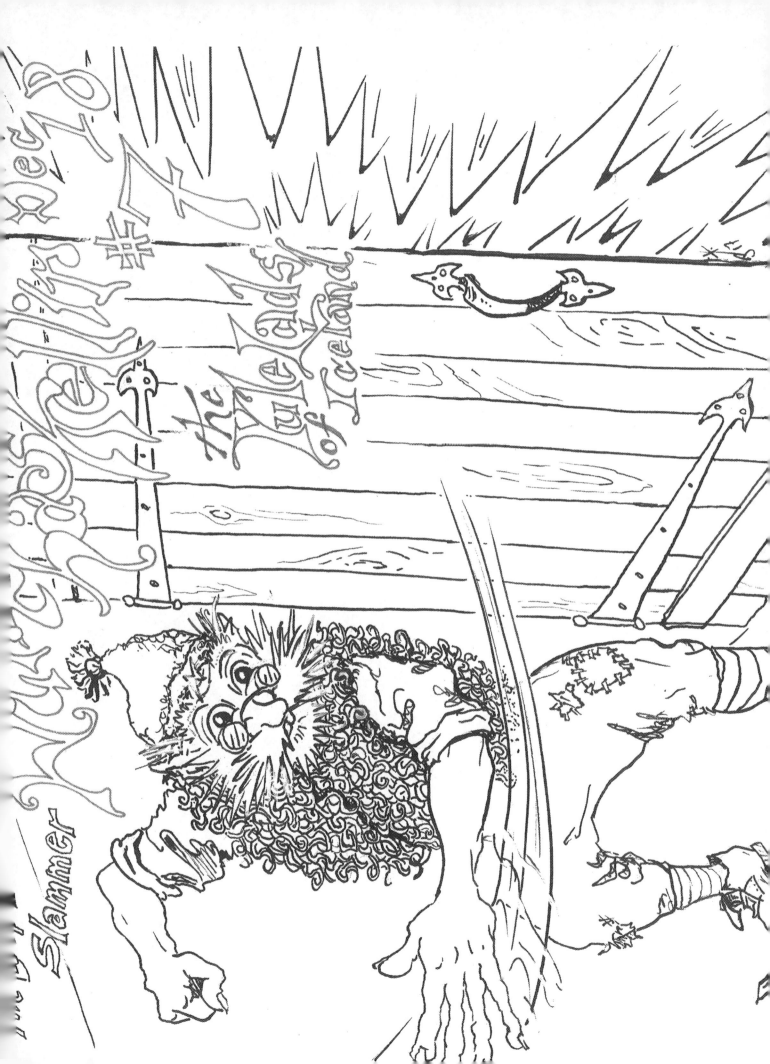

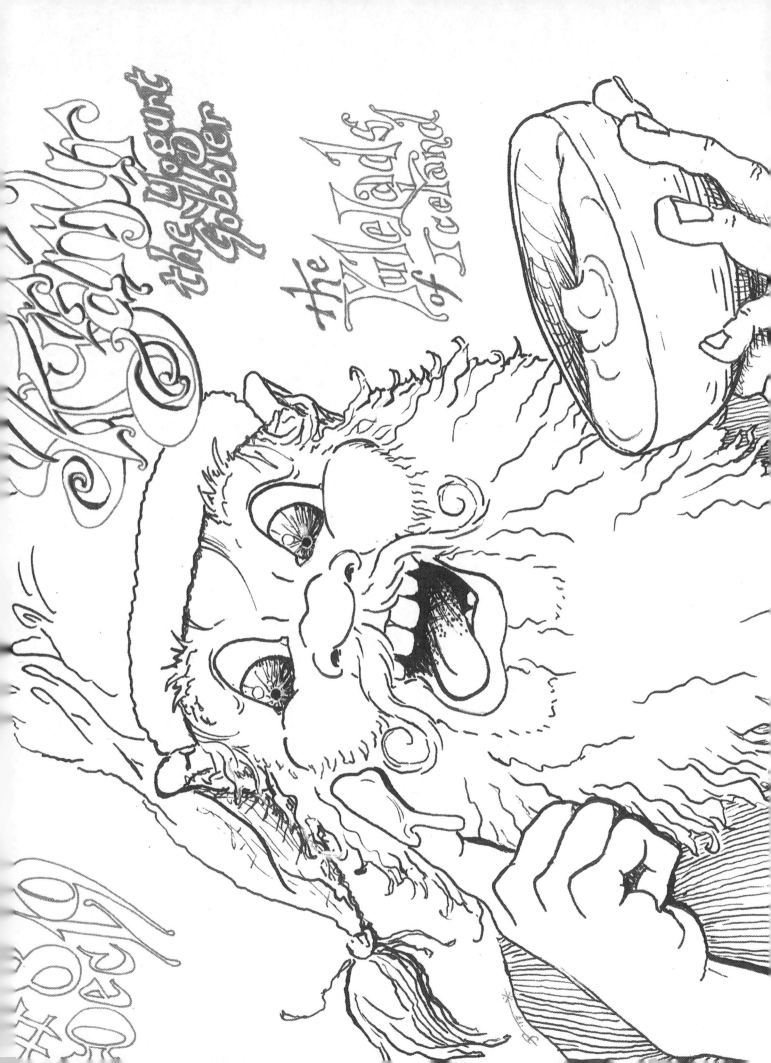

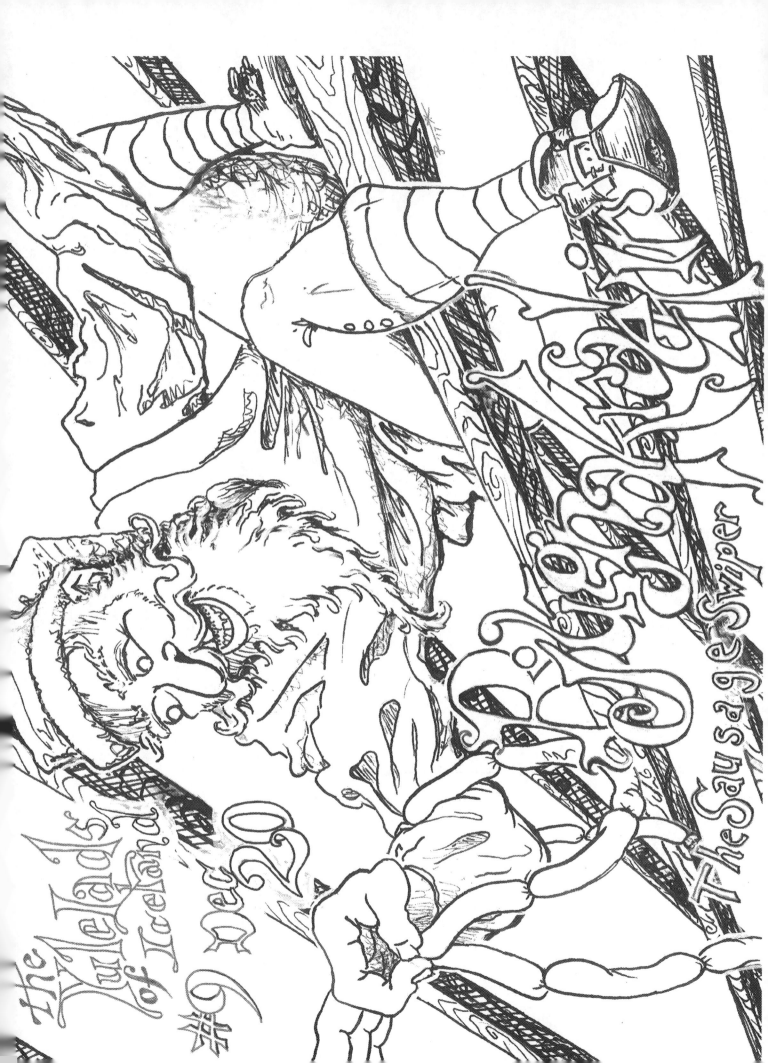

The Yule Lads of Iceland

Dec 20

#6

The Sausage Swiper

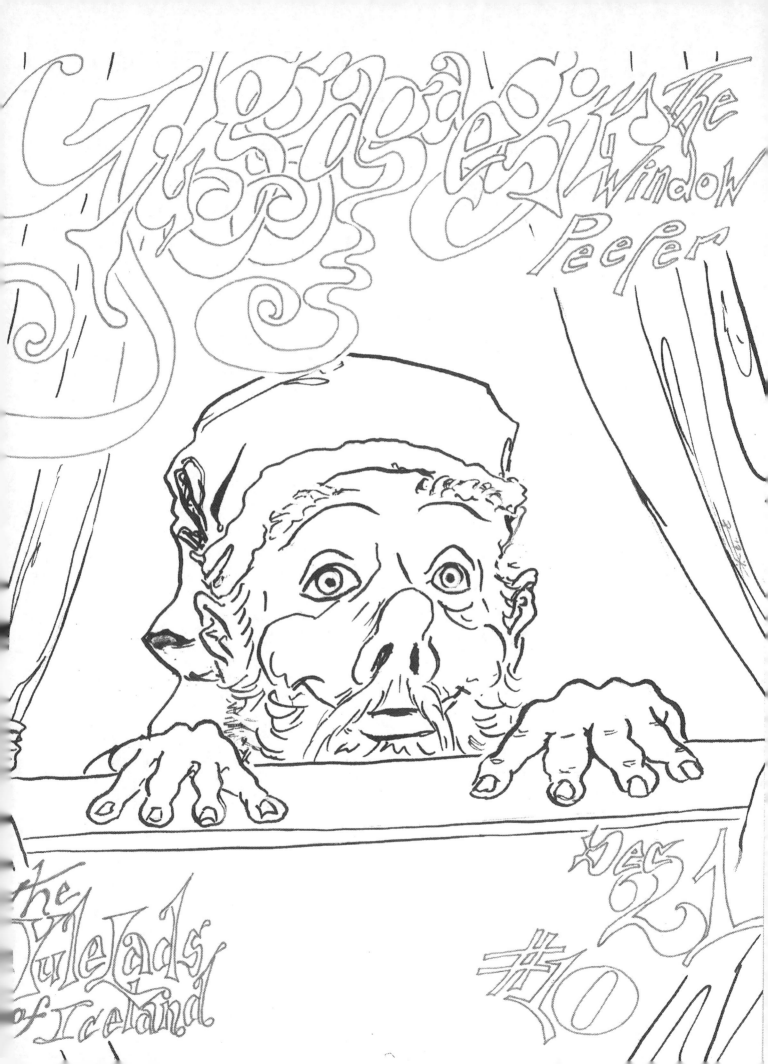

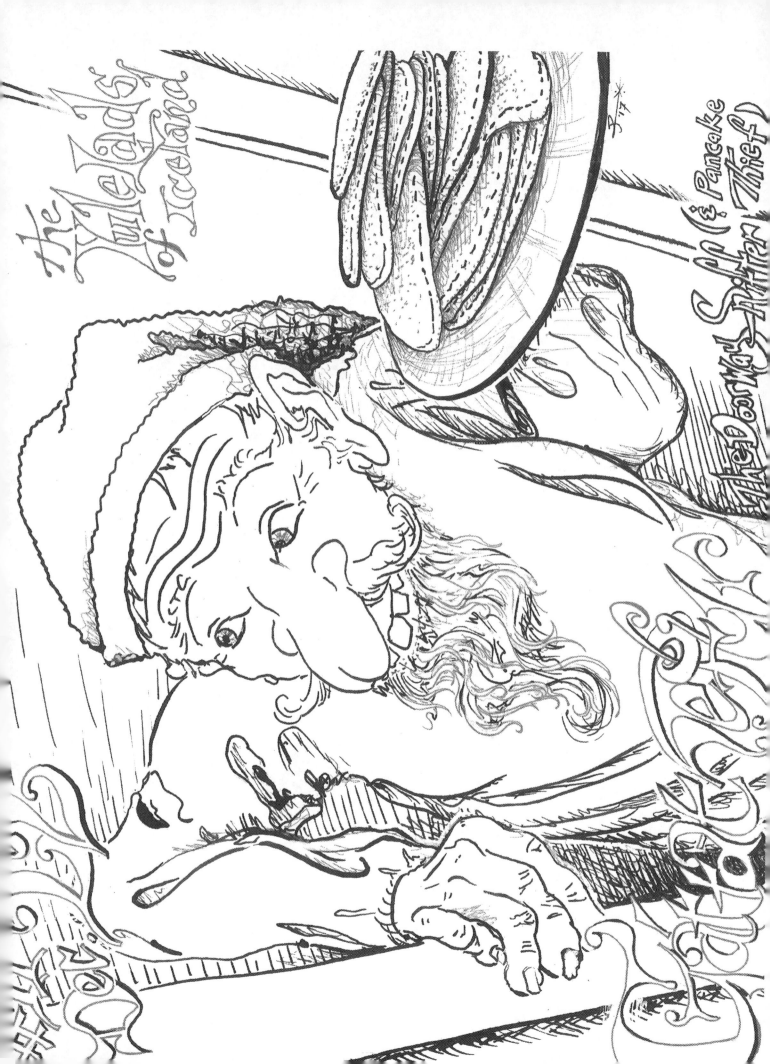

The Yule Lads of Iceland

The Doorway Sniffer (& Pancake Thief)

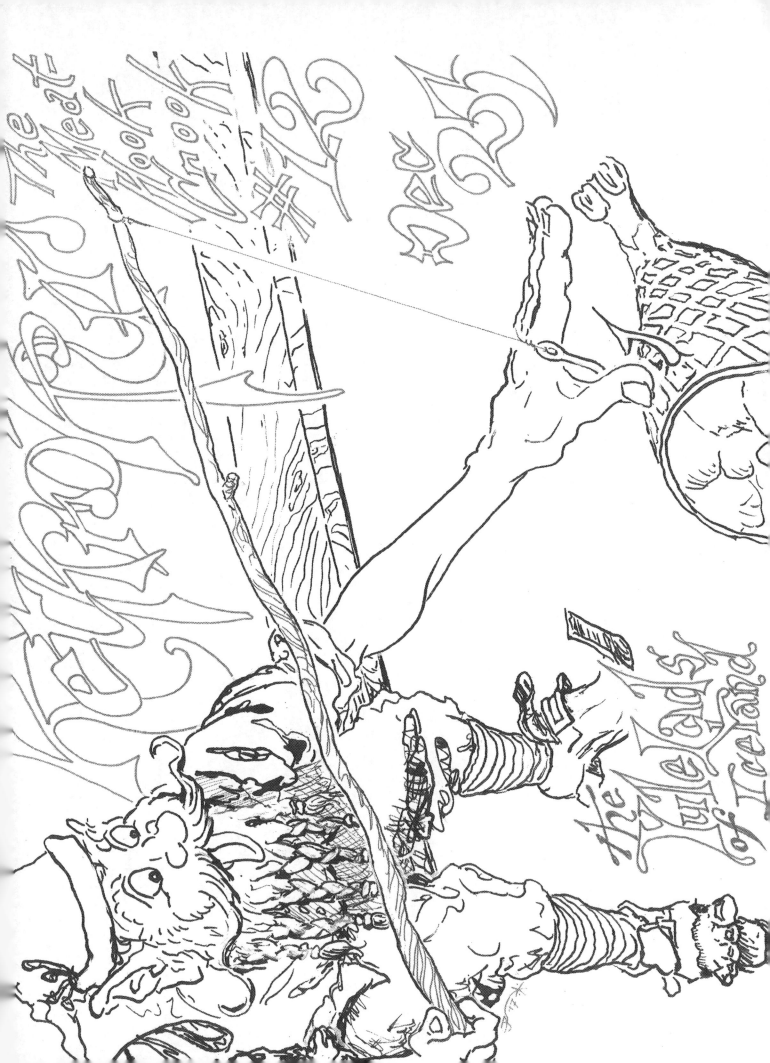

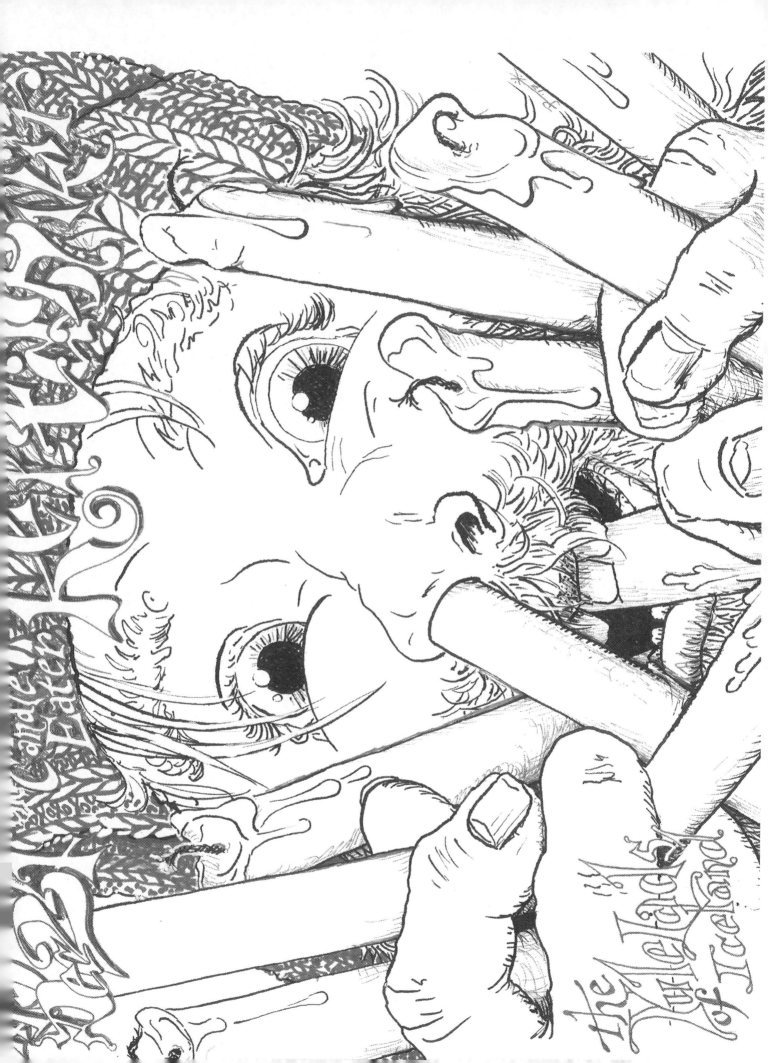

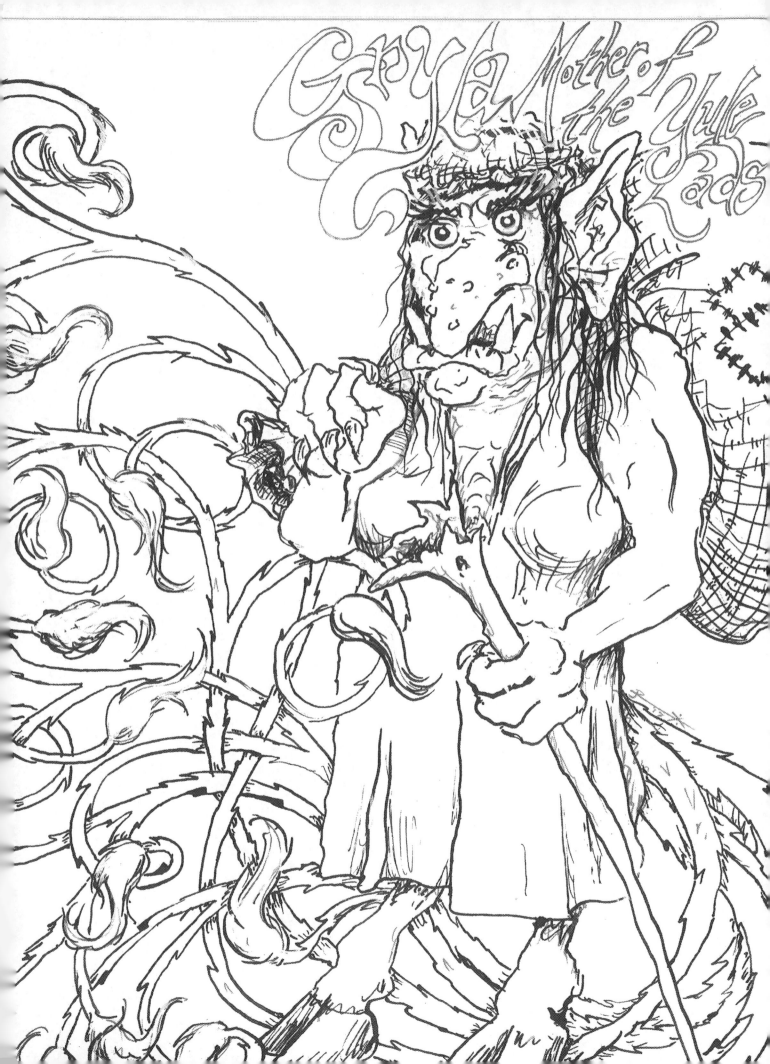

Printed in the United States
By Bookmasters